Essential People Skills

THE FUTURE OF WORK

Essential People Skills

DENNIS MARK

MICHAEL DAM

Marshall Cavendish
Business

Published in 2023 by Marshall Cavendish Business
An imprint of Marshall Cavendish International

A member of the
Times Publishing Group

Other Marshall Cavendish Offices:
Marshall Cavendish Corporation, 800 Westchester Ave, Suite N-641, Rye Brook, NY 10573, USA • Marshall Cavendish International (Thailand) Co Ltd, 253 Asoke, 16th Floor, Sukhumvit 21 Road, Klongtoey Nua, Wattana, Bangkok 10110, Thailand • Marshall Cavendish (Malaysia) Sdn Bhd, Times Subang, Lot 46, Subang Hi-Tech Industrial Park, Batu Tiga, 40000 Shah Alam, Selangor Darul Ehsan, Malaysia

Marshall Cavendish is a registered trademark of Times Publishing Limited

National Library Board, Singapore Cataloguing in Publication Data
Name(s): Mark, Dennis (Information technology consultant) | Dam, Michael (Lecturer), author.
Title: Essential people skills / Dennis Mark, Michael Dam.
Other Title(s): Future of work.
Description: Singapore : Marshall Cavendish Business, 2023.
Identifier(s): ISBN 978-981-5113-81-5 (paperback)
Subject(s): LCSH: Communication in organizations. | Communication in management.
Classification: DDC 658.45--dc23

Printed in Singapore

Contents

WELCOME TO THE FUTURE OF WORK

With all the focus on remote working, automation and the rise of AI, it's easy to overlook possibly the single most important success factor in the workplace: people skills. In the workplace of the future, it is the ability to connect, communicate and collaborate that will allow professionals to create the most value in their work and advance their careers.

Essential People Skills is packed with insights, advice and actionable strategies for developing and applying your people skills in the new economy. From building relationships of trust to negotiating deals and manoeuvring work politics, learn how to stand out from the cubicle drones and create a thriving, resilient network to support your professional growth through the changes ahead.

The Future of Work is a game-changing collection of business books that explore the rapidly evolving landscape of work today. Within the next five years, many jobs will disappear, many will be created, but what is certain is that all will change. The titles in this new series, written by some of the most influential business leaders, thought leaders, practitioners and consultants in the industry, cover everything from business trends and technological innovations, to revolutions in work culture and the critical skills you'll need in order to stay ahead of the curve.

How to Earn Trust

Even though we are in the digital world with a plethora of social media tools, face-to-face interaction between people at work is still the most effective way to collaborate and build strong working relationships. If you work remotely and face-to-face interactions are not practical, having phone conversations or video-conferencing is your next best alternative. Trust is possibly the most important factor in having a good professional relationship. Trust is defined as "firm belief in the reliability, truth, ability, or strength of someone". If your colleagues trust you, you are in a good position to work with them effectively and be able to get things done.

But how do you build and earn trust, especially if you are new to the team, to the organization or to the company? In this chapter, we will cover ideas you can apply to everyday interactions with your colleagues.

- **Meet your commitment.** First and foremost, you must do what you say. This demonstrates your reliability and dependability. It takes a sustained period of effort to earn trust but you can easily lose it. Regardless of how big or small your commitment is, if you commit to deliver a result or do something for someone, you must do your best to meet your commitment and follow through. If you realize that you won't be able to deliver on your commitment, let them know as soon as possible, fully explain and give an alternative option.

My former manager, a Vice President, had a tendency to ask the same person on my team to complete a task for him. After seeing this a few times, I asked him why he did not ask other members on my team. He answered: "Because I know when Julie says yes to my request, I have complete trust that she will get it done on time, and more importantly, done right. I can go away and don't have to worry about it." One other thing to keep in mind before you commit is that you need to consider carefully whether you have the ability and resources to complete the task on time. If you're not sure about the deadline, give yourself some buffer in case of unexpected problems.

- **Honesty.** Simply put, you can keep a secret, honour someone's confidentiality and tell the truth. When you say, "Your secret is safe with me", honour it. Don't use someone's information shared in confidence against them. As a senior product manager working with my operational planning manager, Dan, on a production plan, I met with him to discuss my proposal. After our discussion, Dan agreed that it was a good proposal and he would support it. When I presented my proposal to the management team later, I received push back from the manufacturing executive about the proposal's feasibility. After listening to my explanation, the executive asked Dan for his opinion. Sensing his manager's hesitancy, Dan backed off his support and said he had concerns as well. Needless to say, I lost my trust and respect for him on that day. I confronted him afterward and he wimped out saying he wasn't very sure about his support in the first place. From that point forward, I avoided working with him and when I had to, I proceeded very cautiously.

Having a hidden agenda is something to avoid as well. For example, proposing something that you say will be good for the team when it will only benefit you. As the old saying goes: "Fool me once, shame on you, fool me twice, shame on me." People don't want to look foolish or feel they have been taken advantage of. If your idea benefits both you and the team, explain how that will be a win-win. If you only highlight the benefits to the team, people will either see through it or will find out later. Either way, you lose credibility and trust. You may win this time, but in the long run, you'll find it more difficult to work with people and to achieve success for yourself.

- **Give credit where credit is due.** It goes a long way when you praise or give people credit when they have earned it. It makes them feel appreciated and demonstrates your honesty and trustworthiness. Whether you're a team leader or a team member, focus on the team and not on you. It is better for team members to have others recognize them for their work. When people see that their work is recognized and appreciated, they're motivated and more willing to put their energy to the task at hand. Therefore, you should make a conscious effort to recognize opportunities to reward your colleagues for the job well done. A small gesture goes a long way. Something as simple as complimenting them and recognizing their work publicly during a team meeting or sending a message to their manager will do wonders for earning their trust.

When I was working on data analytics, I received a request from a Senior Vice President to develop an IT tool for him to be able to access any key business metric he wanted. I solicited a couple of strong IT experts to help me with the project. When we presented the tool to him, he was impressed. He knew me but not the two IT specialists. At the end of the meeting, I thanked the team for going above and beyond to help me. When I told the Senior VP that they were the architects responsible for the development of the tool, they were very pleased with the recognition, especially from a high-level senior executive. I earned their trust and felt confident they would be willing to help me again in the future. Even though I did not publicly give myself credit, the Senior VP later told me he appreciated my leadership in recruiting the right people and getting it done quickly and successfully. In this project, I also earned the executive's trust by delivering on my commitment.

- **Maintain your professionalism.** At all times, especially when under pressure, maintain your professionalism. This means you should stay calm, poised, focused on the business issues at hand and not get personal. This is particularly important when you're leading a team or working on a team. During a project, inevitably the team will run into unexpected problems that may cause people to react emotionally. When we are emotional, we tend to get personal instead of focusing on the task at hand, show our tendency to be condescending, sarcastic and to blame other people. If you feel you are getting too emotional, excuse yourself and take a break to calm down. Or if you see others behaving this way, call for a break.

  I saw first-hand an episode in a meeting my former manager attended with his boss and his peers. As he got heated, he made some out-of-character insulting comments about another VP, even suggesting that this VP should be fired. Well, it didn't go over well with the people in the meeting and a few weeks later, he was fired. Although the reason given for the firing was "organizational change", my boss and I knew full well that that was not the real reason for his firing.

- **Listen.** From my experience, I believe that if you are a good listener, people are more likely to trust you. This is because people feel you have taken the time to listen to them, to seek to understand, and are empathetic to their situation. When we fully listen to people, we develop and nurture a safe environment where they can open up and be themselves without fear of judgment. If we honour their confiding in us and keep it confidential, we will earn their trust even more. Take the time and make an effort to listen by asking questions so you can truly hear them. In addition, before you give feedback, seek to understand fully and accurately so you can give specific feedback. And when you do give feedback, focus on giving constructive feedback with examples instead of criticism. Refer to the chapter on "How to be give and receive feedback" for suggestions.

• **Striving to achieve team goals.** If you're leading a team, focus relentlessly on having your team achieve the common goals and persuading them that the team's success defines their success. If the team fails to meet the team goals, everyone fails. There is no room for anyone to feel they can deflect the blame for the team's failure by pointing fingers at other people. When your team sees that you don't have a personal agenda and you drive them to work together to deliver results, they will likely follow your lead. Even if you are a team member and not a leader, you can still play a significant role in helping your leader focus the team on achieving the team goals.

• **Being a good team player.** If you act and present yourself as a team player willing go out of your way to help team members get their work done, people are more likely to trust you. However, make sure you can complete your work before committing to help.

Completing your work is your first priority. It's better not to commit than commit and not deliver. Knowing how to work efficiently will enable you to have time to assist your team. Being a good team player also means recognizing the team's weaknesses, bringing them to attention and finding ways to address them. The team is only as successful as the weakest link in the chain. By proactively addressing the weak spots – whether it's a specific area of the project or someone not delivering quality work – you help the team achieve the best results possible.

- **Seek first to understand.** If your colleague is delivering subpar work and that's hurting the team, seek to understand first and not jump to conclusions. Resist the urge to assume that he's a bad team player who's not fit to be on the team, especially if he has a good track record. There could be many reasons for this situation, such as personal or family issues, or too much work responsibilities that are spreading him too thin. Seek this person out to discover why he's not delivering his best work by listening and asking questions. Chances are he will be open with you if he knows that you sincerely want to help. Once you find out the root cause, then you can explore possible solutions.

When I interviewed my former colleagues for this book, I heard an example from a person I had worked closely with for several years. Mary said during a big project she was working on, there was a team member who was delivering mediocre work results.

There were several unhappy team members who were afraid this would reflect negatively on them. Mary went to this person and expressed her desire to understand what was going on and to help. She came to learn that the team member did not know how to say no to his boss, and as a result, kept getting work added to his plate. He was overloaded with work projects, felt overwhelmed and did just enough to stay above water. Mary helped him approach his manager to explain his situation. Together they helped the manager understand the risks and consequences to the team of not delivering on his commitment due to the heavy workload. The manager understood and removed some of the lower-priority tasks. As a result, he was able to get back on track. He thanked Mary, and from that point on, he was more open to confiding in her and seeking help before it was too late.

- **Socialize.** Get to know your colleagues. We spend so much time trying to get work done that we have little time for socializing, to get to know another side of the people we work with. I was guilty of this early in my career. I didn't spend enough time building personal connections with my peers. Developing and maintaining relationships with my peers sooner would have helped me work with them and get things done more effectively.

Although time is valuable and we never seem to have enough of it to finish our work, make it a priority to get to know your colleagues. Start by showing your genuine care for them as colleagues and as people. Learn about their interests and hobbies outside of work. If you both enjoy the same sport – tennis, for example – invite them to play with you from time to time. Make an effort to have lunch with them instead of eating alone at your desk. Instead of taking a walk by yourself during a break, ask a co-worker to walk with you. And once in a while, organize a group happy hour after work where everyone can enjoy each other's company. This worthwhile time investment will enable people to feel closer and have more trust in you and each other, and help you to work even better with them and get things done more effectively.

How to Communicate Effectively

Verbal

- Build rapport
- Understand before responding
- Focus on meeting objectives
- Listening is key
- Contribute by speaking up
  - Research meeting purpose beforehand
  - Formulate thoughts first
  - Focus on meeting topics
  - Avoid slang/jargon
  - Ask for summary of next steps
- Remote participation
  - Speak clearly and loud enough
  - Ask for clarification/ engagement
  - Engage facilitator to provide "on-site" information, e.g. drawing side discussions

Written

- Professional etiquette
- Guidelines for external correspondence
- Don't burn bridges
- Don't email when upset
- Best practices
  - Brief and to-the-point
  - Summary of key points after meeting
  - Be prepared that your mail is shared/forwarded
- Double-check
  - Re-read before sending
  - Check To and CC lists
  - Spelling, grammar, name

How to Communicate Effectively – Verbal and Written

If I had to pick one skill that separates a star performer from an average employee, it would be communication. Communication is the ability to convey information to other people effectively and efficiently. It is how you articulate your views and opinions clearly and persuasively, either verbally or written. From my experience, it is the number one factor that determines how successful you will be in your job. It is as important to understand as it is to be understood. Far too often in Asia, I notice Asians not being vocal about expressing their thoughts and accepting too easily pushbacks and one-way communication. To go beyond average to outstanding, especially in the context of international benchmarks, you must learn and practise the art of communicating.

WHY IT IS IMPORTANT TO BE A GOOD COMMUNICATOR

When I was a Senior Director at a Fortune 100 company, I had an opportunity to promote one employee on my team. I had two talented candidates who had been delivering excellent results, Robert and Timothy. As part of the process, I solicited input from people who had worked with each of them. Their feedback was consistent that both were dedicated team members who worked hard, met their commitments and delivered excellent results. However, I received very different feedback in the area of communication. For Robert, his peers said he needed to improve his communication skills. Often, he wasn't clear in expressing his points and they had to ask him to repeat or elaborate. Due to this weakness, the team couldn't work very efficiently at times since they had to spend more time clearing up any confusion. In addition, two company executives commented that, when doing a presentation, Robert came across a bit timid and unsure of his recommendations. Timothy, on the other hand, received rave feedback for his communication skills. He expressed his views clearly and persuasively, and asked for and welcomed feedback from other people. Executives commended him for his presentation skills and his ability to get his point across and handle questions. Based on the feedback I received, I decided to recommend Timothy for the promotion. He deserved it and my recommendation was easily approved. If I had recommended Robert, I would have gotten strong pushback from my boss and company executives who favoured Timothy more. I committed to get Robert the necessary resources to help him work on improving his communication skills.

Being a good communicator also enables you to be more productive and efficient. Time is precious and having more time to do your work is a big plus. Moreover, if you are recognized for your communication skills, you will get more opportunities to present to company executives, to represent your company at industry events and customer meetings. Taking advantage of these opportunities is a natural way to promote yourself, gain visibility and enhance your standing in the company.

In today's work environment, both verbal and written communication methods are common. In this chapter, I will cover the best approach and practices for both. While a successful professional must have both strong speaking and writing skills, I would rank verbal communication above written skills. The main reason being that the business world focuses on visible optics – how we look, how we appear, how we carry ourselves, how we speak, how we respond, etc. However, I want to emphasize that mastering both verbal and written communication skills is the best way to achieve success and advance your career. An important criterion of being a good communicator is to have a keen sense of the business culture in the company you work for. This is especially important if you work for a multinational company in the US or a Western country.

VERBAL COMMUNICATION

I believe verbal communication is a more difficult skill to master than written. In speaking, we often have to think on our feet with little time to formulate and articulate our thoughts. Once the words leave our mouths, they are gone and we cannot really take them back. In this section, I'll focus on the skills and techniques to help you gain confidence in speaking up and getting your point across. We'll focus on group settings – team meetings, project meetings, meetings with management, customers and partners. By mastering communication skills in group meetings, you will easily be able to handle other settings, such as one-on-one meetings. Asians tend to be more introverted and are relatively less vocal compared to the West. The education system and social norms in many Asian countries further push students to value teams and not individuals. Particularly if you are interested a career with multinational companies, you need to stand out from the pack to avoid under-selling yourself against international competition.

VERBAL COMMUNICATION TECHNIQUES AND BEST PRACTICES

- Listening is a key part of communication. Excellent communicators I know and have observed over the years are good listeners. Chloe, a friend of mine who is a great listener, told me of a dinner meeting with a client. Through the entire dinner, she spent most of her time listening and maybe ten percent of the time talking. When they said goodbye after the dinner, her client thanked her for an enjoyable evening and commended her for being a great conversationalist, even though for most of the dinner, she just sat back and listened. Most people like to talk about themselves. By listening, we understand their views and that will help us respond more appropriately. In addition, if you are new to a meeting, asking questions and listening to the responses are good ways to build rapport. Oftentimes, we may be listening but not really hearing what the other person is saying.

- Know objectives of the meeting. This helps you ask the right questions and keep everyone in the meeting focused on the right business issue when a discussion goes off track. Sometimes we don't spend enough time making sure the objective is clear with everyone on the team. When problems arise during a project, as they inevitably will, the best way to get the project back on track is to reset and get everyone to focus on the objective the team is trying to achieve.

- Seek to understand before you respond. Use your listening skills here. When you don't understand what someone is saying, ask them to clarify. Something like: "Could you elaborate for me? I just want to make sure I understand your points," or "What I heard you say is XYZ. Is my understanding accurate?" When you want to respond, having a full understanding of their comment will help you respond appropriately. I would be a rich man if I got a dollar for every time I heard someone giving a response to another person, only to have that person say "That's not what I meant."

- Build rapport. Asking for clarification and rephrasing others' comments are also good ways to connect with your co-workers because they show you are interested and engaged in the conversation. This also helps other people feel comfortable engaging with you and giving you feedback on your work. If you're new to the team and are hesitant to ask "dumb" questions, you can preface your question with: "I'm new to this. Sorry if this is redundant, but I was wondering if you could elaborate on that point for me." Also, acknowledge and add to other people's comments. For example: "That's a good point, John. I also would like to add to that..." Again, this shows your interest, engagement and willingness to share feedback and add value to the discussion.

- Contribute by speaking up. Find out the purpose of the meeting beforehand and ask questions relating to the topic. This helps you formulate your thoughts ahead of time so you can contribute to the meeting meaningfully. Having well-thought-out comments gives you the confidence to speak up and helps you gain credibility. One more point – it's important for you to speak up in meetings. If you don't, people tend not to notice your presence. If you don't think you have any valid points to add, ask someone to clarify their points. At least this allows people to see you, hear you and helps you to feel more comfortable speaking up later. Make a habit of speaking in any meeting at least twice, especially when you are in a meeting with your boss or company executives. Since you may not get this kind of opportunity often, it's your chance to be recognized, get visibility and make a good impression with the management team. You may not want to take the risk of looking bad; however, preparing and thinking beforehand on how you want to contribute to the meeting will give you more confidence speaking up in these situations.

When I taught business leadership classes to college students, I invited one of the country's youngest mayors to speak to my class. Rob was a 28-year-old public official serving a second term. Since he wasn't much older than the students, they could relate to him. When he started his political career, speaking was not natural to him and he had to learn to master his communication skills. One advice he gave to the students was to speak up in meetings in order to be noticed. He said: "You must speak up when you're in a meeting with other people. If you don't, nobody knows who you are."

- Focus your comments on the meeting topic. Avoid making your comments personal. Express your disagreement in a professional manner and base your comments on the topic at hand. By focusing on co-workers' actions and not who they are, they will more likely have productive discussions with you. For example: "I believe your analysis needs more supporting data" as opposed to: "You are clueless." This is a bit extreme but you get my point. Acknowledge their comments before expressing your viewpoints. For example: "I understand and appreciate your perspective, but I see the issue a bit differently. Here's why..." Avoid saying: "That is the most stupid thing I've ever heard."

Don't take people's criticism personally. Ask for examples. Even when someone gets personal with you and makes condescending remarks, resist the temptation to lash back. Put the spotlight back on that person by making them focus on the topic and the facts. For instance, if Debbie says: "Your analysis is horrible," you could reply with: "Debbie, can you give me specific details on the part of my analysis you think is bad." This forces Debbie to be specific. If she was putting you down for her own enjoyment, she looks bad in front of others and probably will not repeat that behaviour next time. You put her on notice that she will not be able to get away with such behaviour. If she gives you the specifics, you can thank her and follow up by asking for suggestions on how to improve your analysis.

If the discussion is getting heated and straying away from the meeting's purpose, propose to take the issue offline and discuss later. For example: "Let's not take more time in this meeting. How about we take it offline and talk afterward?"

• Avoid using slang and jargon when communicating with people from different backgrounds whose native language is not yours because it could be confusing to them and can come across as disrespectful.

• Speak clearly and loudly enough, especially if you have a soft voice. This is particularly important in a phone conference or in a meeting with people from different countries with different native languages. It's helpful to ask follow-up questions to make sure everyone understood your comment, such as: "Any question?", "Is that clear?" or "Anything you would like me to clarify?"

- At the end of the meeting, ask for a summary of the meeting's outcomes and next steps. In addition, if you did not run the meeting, ask the meeting facilitator to send out a summary email to everyone after the meeting. This helps ensure everyone is on the same page, and if there was any confusion or miscommunication, this provides a chance to resolve the issue right away.

- Staying actively engaged in meetings is more challenging if you're working remotely and calling in to a meeting. You're not really able to read people's reactions in the room, and if there are side discussions, you probably can't hear them. Moreover, because you're not physically present, people tend to not notice you. To avoid feeling disconnected from the meeting, make sure you speak up at least a couple of times. Ask people to repeat or clarify their comments to make sure you fully understand. Sometimes people are looking at a picture or a graph specifically related to their discussion and you're lost because you can't see what they're talking about. They don't mean to exclude you. They just aren't cognizant of you because you're not physically there. Don't hesitate to interject and ask them to describe it or email it to you; if you wait, the discussion will pass you by and it's too late to revisit later. Better yet, make a point of asking the meeting facilitator to send you the materials to be discussed prior to the meeting.

The next best alternative to attending the meeting in person is via video-conferencing. When you receive the meeting schedule, ask the facilitator to set up video-conferencing if possible. The meeting will be more productive and easier for you and other people from remote locations to participate.

Self-awareness is important in this increasingly international competitive landscape. In the global talent context, Asians are brought up and trained in very polite environments. Working within international multinational companies with a mix of cultural backgrounds, Asians need to calibrate this politeness. I would suggest to *not* wait:

- For your turn to speak

- For questions to be directed at you

- Others to finish all possible points

Staying quiet will be perceived as a lack of ideas or lack of interest. Both do not look good in building a positive personal brand. I have also noticed that in many countries across Asia, education systems are stressing more life skills such as presentation and communication skills. Since English is typically not the native language, Asians could still be at a disadvantage. However, there are specific strengths Asians could leverage to enhance their presenting and communicating skills, such as:

- Using a graphical approach in communicating. To effectively tell a story or convey an idea, use a drawing to complement your speaking. Pre-drawn graphs projected or freehand on whiteboard helps take away the sole attention and pressure on the speaker and their verbal communication. For example, I once observed that a China team's use of a pre-structured storyline along with the graphs helped ease the delivery of content by having the audience focus their attention on the projected storyboard and not the speaker's language ability.

- Injecting your conviction and passion into your delivery. Preparing your state of mind is a key factor to overcome any potential language barrier. Don't be intimidated by the English language just because it's not your native language. It's a tool for communicating and we don't have to be an English expert to be able to express our views clearly. Your content and ideas are at least as equally important. Practise delivering your content clearly and with conviction is key. I remember when I started up the China marketing team, most of them were not familiar with English as a daily business tool. But two of my team members, Rollin and Stella, were particularly passionate about their business ideas and China market insights. So even with their imperfect English, they were persuasive through their willingness to share their views supported by well-thought-out content and conviction. Today, they are well respected for their business knowledge internationally and they converse fluently in both Mandarin and English.

WRITTEN COMMUNICATION

I believe written communication is easier to master than verbal because we have time to think about what to write, review what we wrote and make changes as we wish before sending out. However, you should not have any doubt about the importance of writing skills. Capturing relevant notes from a meeting is critical to ensure everyone is on the same page. All contracts and agreements are written documents. Even the presentations you deliver include written content. Every strategy plan, product plan or marketing plan is a written document. In addition, people we interact with outside our company or co-workers in other countries may prefer to communicate in writing. In this section, I will discuss useful techniques for written communication.

Written communication includes emails, texts, tweets, memos, slides, marketing materials, social media content, etc. A common method of communication in the workplace today is email, especially when discussing business topics. However, given how busy work is, no one has enough time to read through all the emails and memos they receive daily. When we send out a message, we need to be aware of this and make smart use of the recipient's time.

BEST PRACTICES AND TECHNIQUES FOR WRITING

- Professional etiquette I discussed for verbal communication earlier in this chapter applies here as well. You should focus on the topic at hand and not get personal. Avoid being sarcastic, condescending or insulting to the person you are addressing. Even if you send out a critical message, focus on the action that person did and not on their character. Absolutely avoid calling people names. While it may make you feel better temporarily, it can and often will come back to hurt you.

- If you are writing a message when you're upset, do not send it immediately when finished. Wait until you're calmer. Take a short break and then go back to read your message over to see if you want to make any changes. Chances are you will want to modify your original message before you hit the "Send" button.

- Keep your message brief and to the point. People are busy and have short attention spans; each day they probably have to sort through and read hundreds of email messages, not to mention reports and memos. You need to get their attention quickly, so state the objective and key points of your message up front. If the message addresses a complex topic, explain briefly and let them know you will set up a meeting to discuss. You lose their attention with a lengthy message.

- After an important meeting, summarize the key points, decisions, next steps to send to the meeting attendees and other appropriate people. This will offer them a chance to bring up and clarify any unclear issue right away. The written message serves as proof of the decision or agreement, and to prevent unnecessary revisiting of the decision. This helps everyone to be more efficient with their time.

- Re-read your message to make sure you're satisfied with the content. Without fail, whenever I re-read a message, I inevitably find a way to make it more succinct or discover that I had forgotten to include some key information that would strengthen my message.

- Similarly, double-check for spelling and grammar errors. Having spelling errors or grammatically incorrect sentences is sloppy. If you have spent a lot of effort writing a strong message, don't risk weakening it with some careless errors.

- Double-check the "To" distribution list to make sure the recipients are the people you want to send your message to. I have made the mistake of copying and pasting a list of email addresses I thought I wanted to send to. However, after sending the message, I discovered, to my embarrassment, there were people on the list I didn't want to read the message. This can create an embarrassing situation – or worse, ill will – especially if your message is not a pleasant one.

- Don't burn bridges or insult people in your message. Getting even may bring you short-term satisfaction but usually has long-term consequences, especially with people you need to continue to work with. Even if you take it back, it makes little difference since the damage has already been done. Keep in mind your emails can have a long life. Even if you delete your messages later, copies of your messages are stored and may be shared without your knowledge.

- When writing to external parties, follow the company's policy and guidelines. Every company has procedures, policies and format for written documents to external parties. Make sure you are familiar with and follow them. There could be legal or ethical issues if you don't adhere to the guidelines. If your message has potential legal implications, have legal personnel review your message first.

Create Presentation Content

Basics
- Know your audience
- Determine your goal
- Be clear on topic
- Organise into 3 parts:
  - Introduction
  - Main body
  - Conclusion

Design compelling presentations
- Right amount of content
- Prioritize important content
- Put supporting data in backup slides
- 1 key message + 5 bulletpoints per slide
- Use animation to reveal bulletpoints one at a time
- Graphics for impact
- Graphs instead of numbers
- Reinforce with summary to close
- Create flow first; craft words later

Common mistakes
- Unreadable or confusing graphics
- Over-animated slides
- Spelling/numerical errors

How to Create Presentation Content

How well you create and organize your slides plays an important role in your presentation success. The structure, flow and organization of your content are a reflection of your thought process. If the content flow is difficult to follow and the structure is confusing, you will be hard pressed to keep the audience engaged. In this chapter, I'll discuss strategies to organize your presentation slides and to make them compelling. This can be a difficult task as attention span is limited with the many distractions from mobile phones. As a result, we must present the information with focus, a clear story line and key takeaways.

HOW TO ORGANIZE YOUR PRESENTATION

Since slides are commonly used visual materials in presentations, we'll use slides as the presentation format in this chapter. However, there are other formats, such as video, visual props, or just verbal presentation. Regardless of the format you use, the fundamentals for organizing your presentation are the same.

- **Know your audience.** You absolutely should know whom you will be presenting to – your co-workers/peers, company executives, and other workers from different departments or external parties. This will help you tailor your content as well as your style for the target audience. For example, if you present to customers, the look and feel of your slides must be professional and adhere to company standards, and the presentation content tends to gear toward more selling and persuading.

- **Determine the goal of your presentation.** Knowing the goal of your presentation helps you focus on developing the right content and helps you stay on topic during your presentation. Is your purpose to share information, persuade, educate or seek approval? If your presentation is a proposal to management and your goal is to get their approval, your slides will be about why the proposal is good for company business, what the expected results will be and what you need from the executives. On the other hand, if your purpose is to inform, your slides will simply contain the information you want to share, relevant explanation and data you believe your audience wants to know. If your goal is to persuade a customer to be interested in your company's products, your slides will focus on highlighting the benefits of the products and how they will solve the customer's problems better than the competitors. This customer will be front and centre of your slides and your presentation.

- **Be clear on the topic.** This seems basic, but don't assume the audience has knowledge of the topic before they sit down to hear your presentation. If you present new product technology, make sure this is clear at the beginning of the presentation. This helps you keep the presentation on track. When the audience discusses something else or asks questions not related to the presentation, you can draw them back to your topic. For example: "That's a good question. Since it's about a different topic, I don't want to take time away from today's presentation. But I'll happy to discuss that after the meeting. Would that work for you?"

- **Organize the presentation into three parts: introduction, body, and conclusion.** Remember the presentation adage: "Tell them what you're about to tell them. Then tell them. And when done, tell them what you just told them." This is similar to how you would structure writing an essay. In the introduction, you tell the audience your goal for the meeting, the topic you present, set expectations and give any request or expectation you have for the audience. The body is the meat of your presentation. This is where you provide details, explain, expand and support your points. And the conclusion is your chance to summarize the key points you would like the audience to remember.

HOW TO MAKE YOUR SLIDES COMPELLING

Your slides should be easy for the audience to follow, yet intriguing enough for them to want to listen to you. These steps will show you how.

- **Plan for the right amount of content.** Plan to fit your presentation content within the amount of time allocated to you. Plan for an average of four minutes per slide to account for audience questions. For example, if the presentation is for one hour, plan to have no more than 15 slides. People tend to have too many slides for the allotted time. What usually happens is the presenter spends a lot of time on the first few slides and either rushes through the rest or cuts the presentation short because they ran out of time. The audience ends up missing a significant portion of the presentation, and the presenter misses a chance to summarize the key messages for the audience to remember. That is not a successful presentation, and it happens more often than not.

- **Prioritize your content.** If you have a lot of content to cover, prioritize the most important content and put the rest in backup slides that people can review on their own after the meeting. Also put most of the supporting data in backup slides. This will help you manage and pace your presentation better. I would start with an executive summary, a single page capturing the key ideas, recommendations or decisions needed. Depending on the flow, it could be positioned as a closing summary. You should not be surprised that in some cases, five minutes could be the only time you have left to cover your content and this page serves that purpose perfectly. Time management is not a best practice in Asia and overrun meetings are common situations you need to be aware of and accommodate.

- **Keep it simple.** Ideally, you should have one key message and no more than five bullet points for each slide. The slide should get the audience's attention and allow you to expand your point. Using examples to illustrate your points is an effective technique. However, some companies, such as consulting firms, use the practice of putting all the details on the slides. Their reason for this practice is to ensure the audience does not misunderstand or forget any information. This practice is ineffective due to the sheer amount of information that saturates a slide. If you have a lot of information to give to the audience, prioritize and put the secondary or supporting information in backup slides, and let the audience know the details are available for them to refer to.

- **Save the wordsmith for later.** When writing the content for your slides, don't spend too much time trying to phrase perfectly. You want to keep your creative juices flowing and put your thoughts on the slides. Afterward, you can read the slides over and decide what to include, delete or put in backup slides.

Then you can polish your words to get your points across clearly. Since there is limited space on the slide, be succinct and focus on using only appropriate words to convey your points. Don't write sentences as they take up too much space and may confuse the audience. Bullet points are the most effective.

- **Use animation.** If you have several bullet points on your slide and you want to go over each point at a time, animation is an excellent way to manage this. You can reveal the bullet points one at a time, which gets the audience to focus on the one you're talking about and not get ahead of your presentation.

- **"A picture paints a thousand words."** Displaying graphic icons or pictures on your slides is a powerful way to illustrate your message. Graphics can also help make your slides livelier and more dynamic. Slides that only have words can be dull and look uninteresting. However, use your judgment to balance the use of graphics, because too much can distract the audience from the message you want to convey. The use of font colours, size and format can help highlight and emphasize your key messages. However, excessive use of formatting dilutes your message and even distracts the audience from paying attention to your presentation.

- **Show graphs instead of numbers.** If you have a lot of numbers in your presentation, create graphs instead of showing tables. Tables put too much burden on the audience to read and draw their own conclusions. Trend lines, pie charts or bar graphs make it much easier for the audience to understand your message. For example, having a line graph with a trend line showing increasing sales for the past few quarters is far more preferable to a table full of sales figures. It's better to help the audience see your point than requiring them to try to figure it out and risk having them form the wrong conclusion. Too many numbers also run the risk of audience fatigue or unintended discussions in different directions. Avoid numbers that could counter or complicate your story line. Less is more.

- **Include agenda and takeaways.** The first slide should clearly show the purpose of the meeting and the topics you plan to cover. The last slide should have a summary of the key takeaways and if appropriate, a list of the next steps.

- **Run spelling/grammar checks.** More often than not, I've had spelling or grammar errors when creating slides. Taking a few minutes to double-check will save you from potential embarrassment. The errors may also detract from the quality of your slides and make them look sloppy. Since you have invested a lot of time in making your slides as clean as possible, spending a few extra minutes running a spell and grammar check is easy and worthwhile.

COMMON MISTAKES IN CREATING SLIDES

- **Unreadable or confusing graphics.** The audience will spend too much time trying to make sense of your graphics and determine what you are trying to say instead of paying attention to what you are actually saying.

- **Over-animated slides**. Too much animation is distracting. Also avoid using sound effects in a professional meeting environment unless there is a good reason for it. Make a mental note to test your animated slides before you actually present to make sure they work the way you want them to. Avoid dancing or lots of movement animations.

- **Failure to proofread**. As suggested earlier, use spelling/grammar check to correct errors. In addition, make the font size large enough so the audience can read easily, especially for people in the back of the room. Don't try to squeeze in more text on the slides by reducing the font size. If people cannot read your slides, you will lose their attention. Moreover, if you use coloured text or a background, make sure the text is easily readable.

How to Present Persuasively

Presentation skills are an integral component of your overall communication. Regardless of your field of work, you will likely have to present many times in your career. Whether you feel comfortable or not, giving presentations and speaking publicly provide you a great opportunity to shine and get noticed by your co-workers and management. Whenever the opportunity presents itself, take full advantage and make the best of it. Your goal is to make a great impression on these people. The impression you make, or the perception the executives have of you, is based on your presentation performance, good or bad. While this may not seem fair because this could be one of just a few times they see your work, their impression plays an important role in your next performance review and standing in the company.

Moreover, speaking in public is important in a number of activities, including conducting meetings, training sales people, interviewing with the press, meeting with customers, negotiating with company suppliers and representing your company in industry conferences. As a result, being perceived as a good communicator/presenter will open doors to opportunities and serve you well in your career. If you have aspirations to be a high-level

Present Persuasively

Confidence is key
- Build on content expertise

Begin and end well
- Start with focus ideas
- End with summary

Speak loud and clear

Maintain poise and momentum
- Hold off questions/interruptions
- "Parking lots"
- Respond when ready

Engage audience
- Maintain eye contact
- Ask questions to gain participation
- Acknowledge good questions
- For remote audiences, check frequently for signs; pause to re-engage

Improve readiness and skills
- Practice to build confidence
- Get feedback for improvement
- Join presentation training

Common mistakes
- Lack of professionalism
- Distracting gestures/words
- Reading slides to audience
- Misunderstanding purpose of presentation

executive or run a company someday, keep in mind that most, if not all, executives or people in powerful positions have excellent communication skills, especially public speaking.

Some people are natural speakers. Presenting and public speaking seem to come easy to them while others struggle. From observing many outstanding speakers, I firmly believe that this skill can be learned and anyone can be a good speaker, regardless of their personality. I cited Mayor Rob in the chapter on "How to communicate effectively", one of the youngest mayors in the US, who came to speak to my students about his career path and public service. Before Rob became a seasoned politician, he was not great at public speaking. He was a bit shy and tended to be quiet in meetings. Through a lot of work and coaching, he gradually improved his communication skills and became an accomplished speaker. If you see him delivering a speech today, you would think he was a born natural.

Even if you don't think you're a good or natural speaker, embrace the challenge and train yourself to improve. This chapter will show you the techniques and best practices to deliver a great presentation. The goal here is to have confidence in yourself so that when an opportunity arises, you will be excited to volunteer instead of waiting to see if you will be asked to do it while secretly hoping you won't have to. As you continue to improve your public speaking skill, you will feel free to explore future job opportunities without feeling limited by a lack of confidence in your presentation skills.

Regardless of your audience – whether it is co-workers, company executives, internal partners or external parties – there is a set of best practices you can follow to deliver a successful presentation.

HOW TO CONDUCT YOUR PRESENTATION

Equipped with a well-organized and compelling content package, now the time comes for you to present. It is natural to have butterflies in your stomach. The key to handling nervousness is confidence. You must believe you are the content expert and you know more about the topic than anyone in the audience. They should not have more knowledge about the topic than you. Otherwise, you wouldn't be presenting. This belief will give you confidence and also motivate you to prepare the content thoroughly and to practise your presentation until you feel fully prepared. Another confidence booster is to develop a passion for the topic. Subject matter expertise combined with passion for the topic would come across as authentic communication instead of a "canned" presentation. If you are prepared, your confidence will enable you to deliver an outstanding presentation. Below are the best practices you can use.

- Start the presentation by telling the audience what you will cover, then proceed to tell them, and then wrap up by telling them what you just told them. Wrapping up allows you to summarize the main ideas you want the audience to remember.

- Maintain eye contact with the audience and engage them. This can be accomplished by asking questions to get the audience to participate. Start the presentation with a lighthearted joke to break the ice or a quiz question about your presentation to have the audience take a stab at the answer. During the presentation, when you finish making a key point or before moving on to the next point, ask: "Is this clear? Do you have any questions?" This offers the audience opportunities to comment. If you have a colleague in the audience, a good technique is to have them ask a question that will allow you to elaborate. Many people don't want to be the first one to ask a question but once somebody does, they tend to follow. Moreover, don't just read from the slide. Use the slide as a guide for you to expand on and give examples. If you spend most of your talk looking at the slides, you disengage from the audience and create an impression that you may not know your material well.

- Speak clearly and loudly enough for everyone to hear. Make it a practice to ask the audience before you start if they can hear you. When speaking publicly, speak louder than normal so people can hear clearly without having to strain. In addition, when we are a little nervous, we tend to speak faster than usual. Be aware of this and slow your pace down a bit. A good technique to maintain your voice and speaking pace is breathing. We sometimes forget to breathe under the excitement or pressure, and that can negatively affect our ability to control our voice.

- Maintain your poise and don't let questions rattle you. If you're not clear on the question, ask the questioner to repeat: "I just want to make sure I understand your question, can you repeat it for me?" If you don't know the answer to a question, no need to panic. You can say: "I don't have the information off the top of my head. I'll find out after this meeting and get back to you." If you're not ready to give your opinion on a question, buy time by saying: "Good question. I'd like to give it some thought and get back to you." This allows you time to think in the back of your mind while maintaining your composure. When you're ready to answer, you can then get back to that person.

- Remember to acknowledge the audience's good questions or comments. For example, you could say: "That's an excellent question", before proceeding to answer. This connects you to the audience and motivates them to participate.

- Put unrelated issues in the "parking lot". If and when other topics come up during your presentation, resist diving into them, even if your audience wants to, because these issues will distract from the purpose of your meeting and take up valuable time from your presentation. A good technique to handle this without offending your audience is to "park" the issue – capture them on the whiteboard for offline discussion. Your audience is satisfied the issues are noted and will be addressed later, and you are happy to continue with your presentation.

- Wrap up the meeting by summarizing the key points. If there are action items, summarize them with the names of the people responsible for those action items. If the objective of the meeting is to get approval, confirm if you have the approval. If the management team is not ready to make a decision, ask for a timeline you can expect to hear from them or the next step.

- Remember to practise giving the presentation in front of the mirror. Or record yourself on video. Speak as if you're presenting in real time. It may be a bit awkward at first to see yourself, but you can get useful feedback on what you need to improve. You can also practise in front of your friends or family members, who can give you direct feedback. Don't rush into the meeting without rehearsing your presentation. You worked hard to create your slides and develop compelling content, so don't leave it to chance on the most important step – delivering your presentation. Even practising just once is beneficial. Some people prefer framing their presentation as a "story" for practice and having a conversation with their friends instead of actually presenting to them. I find that rehearsing my presentation as if it were real works better for me. Use whatever technique works best for you and remember: you are the expert. Be confident.

- Get feedback on your presentation performance from your manager or co-workers who are good presenters and were present at the meeting. Consult with people who will give you objective feedback. Ask what they liked and didn't like about the presentation, what else they would have liked to see and where you can improve.

- If your company offers presentation classes where you can be recorded on video, take advantage of the opportunity. Given your busy schedule, it can be inconvenient to take time out from work, but make this a priority and it will provide a long-lasting benefit to you.

- If you are presenting to a remote audience over the phone, there are a couple of additional points to remember. If you cannot see the audience's reaction, you have to use your verbal skills to gauge the audience's response and feedback. You need to pause more during your presentation to check for their understanding and solicit questions to avoid misunderstandings. If your manager is in the audience, ask your manager to be your eyes and to help getting the audience to engage. Moreover, the manager can help reset the meeting and pull people back to the topic of the presentation if they get off on a tangent. Before wrapping up the meeting, confirm the key takeaways, next steps and address any disconnects that may arise. If there are open issues, make sure you assign owners for these action items and deadlines to resolve.

- Prepare and have a response plan for some common disruptions:

  ▷ Presentation time suddenly cut short due to schedule changes. Very common with customers or company executives. See the next chapter, "How to communicate and present to specific audiences".

  ▷ Before your meeting starts, emotions can spill over from the previous session. Be alert to this and if you sense it, wait for everyone to calm down and reset before you begin.

  ▷ Leading questions from the audience that aim to get you off track or off balance. Park the questions and pull them back to your main topic.

COMMON PRESENTATION MISTAKES

- Lack of professionalism. Failure to dress professionally or appropriately. If you are presenting to customers, don't come in jeans and t-shirt unless that is what the customers are comfortable with. When in doubt, dress businesslike to show respect. This goes without saying, but you must avoid exhibiting unprofessional demeanour such as appearing intoxicated, making off-colour jokes, being sarcastic or condescending to the audience. These are not only unacceptable but can get you in serious trouble.

- Distracting gestures or movements. Gesturing during a presentation is a good thing, but dancing, or repetitive, distracting gestures and movements detract from your message. Again, recognizing your audience and remembering the purpose of your presentation will help you act appropriately.

- Distracting filler words such as "and", "um", "ah" and "basically". Everyone uses these sometimes and it is fine to use them from time to time, but try to limit the frequency. When it's repetitive, it becomes a distraction.

- Reading to your audience. If you put everything you have to say on your slides and just read to your audience, you might as well just email them the slides and they can read them on their own time. Moreover, try not to use notes or note cards because they encourage reading and discourage eye contact with your audience.

- Misunderstanding of the purpose of your presentation between you and the decision-makers. Make sure everyone is on the same page on the topic and objective of the meeting before you deliver your presentation. This happens more frequently than you think. To prevent this, send an email confirming the purpose of your meeting to the audience prior to your presentation date so any confusion of the meeting objective can be cleared up immediately.

How to Communicate and Present to Specific Audiences

Before proceeding with this chapter, read the chapters on "How to create presentation content" and "How to present persuasively" first if you have not, since that content complements the material here. While the techniques described in those chapters are relevant to all audiences, specific audiences also have their own unique characteristics, which you should be aware of and tailor your presentation to. This chapter covers various audiences you may encounter, their differences and how best to address them.

COMMUNICATING AND PRESENTING TO EXECUTIVES

I have had many opportunities to present to company executives as well as observing first-hand how they conduct themselves in

How to Communicate and Present to Specific Audiences

Executives

Impatient
May cut meetings short

→ Organize content to be adaptable on the fly

→ Keep content succinct, clear and at executive level

→ Be clear on meeting's objective

→ Confirm amount of time available

→ Balance between executive discussion and meeting goals

→ Get a champion ready to support

Customers

Like to be heard
Big investment of time

→ Be clear on meeting's objective

→ Know who you are meeting with

→ Balance between company advocate and being honest

→ Be careful with confidential information

→ Be careful about making commitments

→ Maintain professionalism with upset customers

Third parties

Similar to customers

→ Contract agreement and negotiation

→ Read Chapter 19 on being a good negotiator

→ Legal review of contract

International audiences

Differences in language, business culture, etc

→ Be aware and sensitive of differences

→ Speak at the audience's pace

→ Work with a translator

→ Avoid jargon, slang, acronyms

→ Make use of visual aids

→ One-on-one follow-on meetings

meetings. I also have heard well-known Chief Executive Officers (CEOs) of multinational companies talk about their expectations when attending presentations. Here's a summary of what I learned.

- **Limited available time.** Company executives normally have a tight schedule. Usually you have a short amount of time (30–60 minutes) to meet with them, depending on the topic and objective of the meeting. They are unlikely to extend your meeting time because they typically have other meetings scheduled already. As a result, you must prepare your content to be able to finish your meeting within the allotted time while also achieving your meeting goal, especially if it's a meeting where you need a decision from them.

- **Possible interruptions and meeting time reduced.** It's not unusual for your meeting to be shortened due to the executive team getting interrupted by other matters or if they decided to extend the meeting prior to yours. This can be a real-time decision you need to make just before your meeting begins or worse, during your meeting. Therefore, you need to be prepared to handle these unexpected situations and still be able to accomplish your goal.

- **Impatience.** Patience is not their strong suit, given the demands on their time and attention. They don't tolerate unclear meetings where they don't know the meeting's purpose or what is expected of them. They tend to lose their patience if the meeting gets sidetracked or if they're not getting answers to their questions. The irony is that sometimes the executives can get the meeting off track by their own discussion with each other. While they like to see a well run, disciplined meeting from you, they sometimes are not disciplined and need to be guided back to the topic at hand. You need to be aware of this and prepared accordingly.

Here are the keys to preparing your content and conducting presentations.

- **Organize your content to be able to adapt on the fly.** Since you likely will have more material to cover than the time allowed, prioritize the content that the executives care most about. Also, allocate time for questions and discussions from the executives. Keep in mind the rule of thumb of having one slide for every four minutes of meeting time. If it's a 60-minute meeting, have no more than 15 slides. Put other more detailed slides in backup in case you need to refer to them. In addition, organize your presentation slides into modules so if you need to, you can prioritize and use the most important modules first and leave other details for the executives to review later at their convenience.

- **Keep your content succinct, clear and at the right level.** How well you do this determines how likely you and the executive team can stay on track and finish the meeting as you hope. Adhering to having one slide for every four minutes will help you accomplish your meeting goal. However, this doesn't mean you should cram as much detail as possible into every slide. We have a desire to show how extensive our work is and are afraid we may leave out something important that executives care about. Avoid the urge to do this.

You should have one key message for each slide you want your executives to remember. Many executives are data-driven and the more data you show, the more likely they will drill down and not able to see the forest from the trees. If this happens, your meeting is at risk of getting derailed. Moreover, you don't want your analysis to be questioned since it is your job to make sure it's thorough and to deliver the key conclusions you want the executive to keep in mind. If they question your analysis, it brings your credibility into question and will cloud your overall meeting goal.

There is one story in particular I would like to share with you that still brings a smile to my face whenever I think about it. As a manager leading a team of marketing professionals in my company's server business unit, I normally reviewed my team's presentations before they presented to the management team. Before one important business review meeting with our General Manager and Marketing Vice-President, I reviewed the presentation slides from my employee, Elaine. Elaine had done an extensive and thorough analysis, but put a great deal of detail on already crowded slides. I suggested to Elaine to "dumb it down" and simplify her slides so the executives could understand. Well, during her presentation, our GM, a brilliant executive who had a tendency to drill down on numbers, started asking detailed questions and getting into a rat hole with Elaine. After getting a few questions too many, she stopped her presentation and said to him: "Well, I had all the details on the original slides to show you, but my manager told me to keep it really simple because otherwise you won't get it." I felt like hiding under the desk. Fortunately, I had a good enough relationship with the GM and he laughed it off because he recognized his data-driven tendencies. He understood that we wanted to high-light the key points for him and the Marketing VP to make decisions instead of using their valuable time to talk about the numbers.

- **Be clear on your meeting's objective.** When you start your meeting, this is the first thing you should cover. You need to state clearly the purpose of the meeting and more importantly, what you want from them. Do you need them to make decisions on your proposal? Do you need them to provide their input and guidance on your project? Or are you there to only give them updates and share information? This will prepare their mindset for the meeting since they probably have not seen your presentation materials.

- **Confirm the amount of time you have.** Confirm this at the beginning of the meeting even if you had been told earlier how much time you have. If you learn you have less time now, adjust in real time to make sure your meeting agenda fits into the time constraint. And even if you have confirmed the time at the start of meeting, your time could still be cut short by unexpected events. However, if you had organized your content as we discussed above, you are prepared to handle these unexpected interruptions.

- **Balance between executive discussions and achieving your meeting goals.** In your meeting, the executive team may become animated and get into lengthy discussions with each other. While it's important for them to talk and think through the information to help them make decisions, you need to determine whether the discussion focuses on the meeting topic or on another unrelated topic. I have seen numerous meetings where the discussion evolved from the original topic to something completely different. Also keep in mind some executives may not be disciplined about staying on topic. Moreover, be aware of the politics at play because some of the executives may be trying to score points with the CEO.

If you see the discussion getting off track, look for an appropriate time to interject and remind the executive team to get back on topic. A good time could be when an executive finishes their thoughts. You can be polite but firm by saying: "Sorry to interrupt, but we only have 20 minutes left in this meeting and we have quite a bit of material to cover. Can I continue?" Or if they seem to be in the middle of some serious discussion, you can suggest: "Sorry to interrupt, but we only have 20 minutes left in this meeting and we have quite a bit of material to cover with you and I would like to continue, or would you like me to schedule another time?" Chances are they will ask you to continue. You may need to do this a couple of times throughout your presentation to keep the meeting on track. This is also a good way to show your leadership ability.

- **Have a champion to support you.** This can be your manager who is high enough on the management chain relative to the executives, or this can be one of the executives you and/or your manager have a good relationship with. With this executive, try to have a little bit of time beforehand to give her an update, your recommendation and most important, to ask for her support. She can play a pivotal role in providing you support and "air cover" during the meeting. Because of her status and credibility, she can help placate other executives who may have concerns about your recommendation. If you have an important decision-making meeting, try your best to meet with the key stakeholders prior to meeting to get their buy-in or at least to understand what issues they may have. This will help your meeting go smoother and minimize surprises.

There will be times when you're attending a meeting but not presenting, and in these cases, you don't need to be as prepared as the presenter. However, since it's not often you get a chance to be in a meeting with key executives, you should view the meeting as an opportunity for you to participate intelligently, contribute to the discussion and gain visibility. In order to do this, yes, you need to spend a little time to prepare.

- Know the purpose of the meeting. This provides you some ideas for your participation. If the meeting is to make a decision, you can play a role in making sure there is closure – a decision is made or clear next steps are understood. In certain meetings, especially difficult ones, people are reluctant to make decisions and the presenter or meeting facilitator is hesitant to push the executives for an answer. If you see this situation, you can speak up to remind everyone of the objective of the meeting and the importance of reaching closure. People will respect you for your assertiveness. No one wants to come out of a meeting confused or unclear about the outcomes or next steps.

- Know your role in the meeting. If you are responsible for the content of a particular agenda item, prepare to provide insights even if you're not presenting, or to answer potential questions from the executives. If you don't have the agenda, ask the presenter/meeting facilitator so you can anticipate potential areas where you can speak up and add value to the meeting.

- Be ready to provide support to the presenter or other team members. This is a natural way to gain credibility and visibility at the same time. Presenting under the spotlight can be stressful and rattle anyone, especially when facing tough questions. This is where you can help. If the presenter seems unsure about the answer or doesn't seem to have the information to a question and you do, you should volunteer and give your answer. The presenter will appreciate your help and the executives will be impressed with your knowledge and teamwork. You do need to keep in mind the balance between stepping in to help out and showing up the presenter. If you repeatedly chime in, you come across as overbearing, especially since you're not the focus of the meeting.

- Asking questions to get the presenter to elaborate on certain points is another way to provide support. Oftentimes in the heat of presenting, the presenter or meeting leader may forget to elaborate on certain important points. By asking them to elaborate, you help them slow down and stress the key points. Something as simple as saying "To the point you just mentioned, can you elaborate and provide more detail?" would serve as a trigger for the presenter to expand their point. Throughout my career I have used this technique many times with my peers and my team members and they very much appreciated my gesture. Many of them have asked me to play this role for them when they had important presentations.

- Speak up once or twice even if you have no visible role in the meeting. Obviously you should make comments relevant to the meeting. Many times we don't speak up because we're afraid to ask stupid questions or say something silly. However, asking for clarification is a good and safe technique to use. For example, if an executive makes a comment that's unclear to you, you should ask the executive to elaborate. For example, "Can you elaborate on that point a little more? I just want to make sure I understand" is a perfectly acceptable response. Some people in the meeting are likely to have the same question but were afraid to ask and would appreciate that you did.

COMMUNICATING AND PRESENTING TO CUSTOMERS

If you have a chance to meet and interact with customers, take advantage of the opportunity. You can gain great insight about the customer's business and their challenges. You can read reports about customers but nothing hits home quite like meeting them in person and talking to them directly.

- **Customers like to be heard.** Customers frequently have business challenges they need to address in order to improve their company's performance. When they meet you, they like to talk to you about their challenges and look to you as a source of information that potentially can help them. Moreover, if customers have some issues with your company's service and products, they will definitely want to let you know.

- **Big investment of time.** Whether they come to visit at your company's site or vice-versa, it's a significant investment of their time and resources, and as result, they have specific objectives and expectations in meeting you. You probably also have specific needs you want to get from them. Therefore, it's important to understand their objectives and balance those with yours to make sure both parties get what each wants from the meeting.

- **You are your company.** When you meet the customer, they see you as representing your company. They don't see you as an engineer in the engineering department or customer support representative or product manager. They don't look at you as only having specific responsibilities for your job. When I visited and presented to customers, they didn't see me as a Product Management Director responsible for hardware products. They saw me as my company's representative and would feel free to discuss anything relating to their business with my company. When you meet them and if they have a request or demand, they will ask you and expect you to follow through.

Here are the keys to preparing your content and conducting presentations:

- **Be clear about the objective of your meeting with the customer.** As with meeting with executives, find out the customer's objectives for the meeting, their issues, topics they want to discuss, etc. The customer Sales Representative (SR) or Account Manager (AM) is a great resource to find out. Most SRs or AMs will contact you to let you know ahead of time about the meeting details. They have a vested interest in keeping their customer happy and making sure they get what they come for.

If you don't hear from the sales team, get in touch with them prior to the meeting to get all the information you need so you can properly prepare. As importantly, when you meet with the customer, confirm the agenda and topics with them. Ask questions to find out what is top of mind, what issues they are facing, what they want to discuss and what their expectations are. Between the time of your meeting with the sales team and your meeting with the customer, they could have met with other competitors and learned new information they want to discuss with you.

- **Know whom you are meeting with.** Different companies may have different representatives meeting you, including technical people (IT managers, system administrators, CIO) and business people (purchasing managers, business line managers, CEO). Knowing whom you will meet and what they have in mind helps you determine if you need to invite other experts from your company to cover topics that you don't have the expertise on. In the course of briefing with the sales team, you can also learn if there is someone from the customer company who is a champion for your company – someone you can count on to support you in the meeting.

- **Balance between being the company advocate and projecting honesty.** While customers understand you are there to advocate and promote your company, they do not expect you to be just a talking mouthpiece for your company. You will earn respect and credibility if you are objective about the strengths and weaknesses of your company's products or services while promoting your company at the same time. They don't expect your company's products or services to be perfect but they do want to know about any product issues and how your company is addressing them. In particular, if they hear from one of your competitors pointing out the weaknesses of your product or services, they would definitely want to validate the credibility of the competitor's claims.

  A common place where customers want objectivity is in comparing your company versus your competitors. Customers realize every company wants to differentiate themselves from others, but what they look for is whether the comparisons are credible and can be validated. As a result, you will earn the customer's trust and gain credibility by balancing between being an advocate for your company and being objective in your assessment of potential solutions to solve their problems. However, before you give your opinion, make sure you listen and ask a lot of questions so you have a clear understanding of what they heard as well as their own perception. I have seen instances where my company's presenter turned the customer off and lost their interest by being in complete selling mode regardless of what the customer was saying.

- **Be cautious with confidential information.** Customers are interested to hear about your company's future strategy and product roadmap so they can plan accordingly. Since much of your company's future plan is confidential, exercise caution. Customers typically sign a non-disclosure agreement (NDA). However, even with an NDA, proceed with caution. If the customer is a loyal customer and has a good track record with your company, it may be fine to share confidential information with the confidence they would not divulge it to your competitors. My rule of thumb, especially with customers I'm not sure about, is to assume that whatever information I share, confidential or not, will get into the hands of my competitors.

- **Be careful about making commitments.** Oftentimes customers will take advantage of the opportunity to ask for certain commitments – for example, commitment for a date to fix a problem, to deliver a replacement product, to provide a new software upgrade, to provide longer support to discontinued products, or to give special pricing. Unless it is within your power and you are sure it's the right thing to do and you can deliver on your promise, do not commit. Although you may feel a lot of pressure to agree to the request, especially if you have an unhappy customer, resist the urge. It's worse if you cannot deliver and, trust me, the customer will hold you to it. Instead, commit that you will take the request back to the company to have the right person work on the request and get back to them. You must follow through on this commitment.

- **Maintain your professionalism when facing an upset customer.** Sometimes you may get blindsided by an unhappy customer with issues you were not aware of. On one of my customer visits, I wanted to discuss with the customer about our future printer technology. Prior to the meeting, I had a briefing with the account Sales Representative and no issues or concerns came up. When a co-worker and I arrived at the customer site to meet them in a conference room, they proceeded to lay into us about the problems they had and their dissatisfaction with our company. We sensed their frustration and anger as the volume of their voices got louder. We were caught completely by surprise and worse, the SR was nowhere to be found and he never warned us about the customer issues.

We were clueless because their issues were related to the computer business unit and not our printer business unit. However, we realized that we represented our company, not just the business unit we worked in. There was only one thing we could do. We sat down and listened patiently. We did not even attempt to mention the reason for our visit. We asked questions to make sure we captured their problem accurately. When they finished venting and giving us a list of things they wanted answers on, my colleague calmly thanked them for their feedback. Then he explained that we were not aware of the issues beforehand, and although we were not directly involved in these issues, we would make sure that the appropriate people would get back to them. We committed to them that we would personally let them know who their contact would be.

After the customers calmed down, I asked them if I could take a little bit of their time to show them a new printer technology and get their feedback to help us design the right product. They agreed, listened attentively and actively gave us feedback. They ended up talking with us for another hour. The moral of the story here is that when we meet customers, we are our company's spokespersons, we listen to their needs and concerns, and we take ownership to follow through with them.

COMMUNICATING AND PRESENTING TO THIRD PARTIES

Third parties include suppliers who provide your company with materials to produce your products, contractors who perform services for you such as programming or creating marketing plans, partners who team up with your company to provide solutions, or distribution partners who market and sell your company's products.

- While this relationship is different than that between your company and customers, the discussion points on customers are applicable here as well – confidentiality, understanding the other side's perspective, the need to listen, etc.

- One area I want to emphasize is regarding contract agreement and negotiation. Usually it takes many meetings to negotiate an agreement on how the two companies will work together and what to commit to. Don't rush or get pushed into an agreement. Take your time to understand the other party's issues and needs as well as explore all possible options in order to arrive at a win-win agreement. Moreover, don't commit to an agreement unless you have full authority on the final contract and you're confident about the terms and conditions. Review the terms with your manager and other experts in the company to ensure you have covered all the bases. Finally, have the legal department review the contract. This review process can be lengthy but it's better to take this step to avoid any legal issues or liability in the future.

COMMUNICATING AND PRESENTING TO INTERNATIONAL AUDIENCES

This applies to company employees and customers, as well as partners in other countries who have different native languages, customs and business cultures. The points we've discussed in this chapter apply to these audiences too. In addition, I'll focus on the unique characteristics of these audiences and how to present to them.

- **Be aware and sensitive to their differences.** These include differences in language, business culture and customs. The more you understand the unique differences and how to work effectively with them, the more successful you will be. For example, if English is not your native language, you have an accent and you are presenting to a group of American people, remember to speak louder than your normal speaking voice and speak slower to make sure that they can understand what you're saying clearly. Culturally, people in other countries may not be as direct as Americans. For example, Japanese customers are polite and tend to listen and not ask a lot of questions in public. Moreover, they're not comfortable saying no, even if they cannot commit to your request. Silence does not mean yes. It's prudent to confirm in writing all agreements before proceeding.

- **Speaking at a pace that works for your audience.** As suggested above, speak a little bit slower and louder to make sure your audience can follow you. This is true especially if you are a fast speaker or have a soft voice. After every key point, pause and ask for understanding and anything the audience wants you to repeat or elaborate. This will ensure that the audience understands what you say. Don't assume the audience understands. Americans are more straightforward and will ask you to explain or repeat if they don't understand, but Asian people are subtler and don't want to interrupt you. So remember to double-check.

- **Learn to work with a translator.** In your speaking engagements, you may have a translator to interpret for the audience. This can be a bit awkward since it doesn't promote a smooth presentation. However, you should plan your presentation to accommodate the translator if there will be one. Meet with the translator prior to your talk to brief her on your topic and give her a quick overview of your presentation. Also work with her on how to coordinate the presentation, including where you should pause for the translation. Some translators prefer short sentences or one message at time while others can handle multiple points at a time. Syncing up and coordinating with the translator will make your presentation delivery more seamless to the audience.

- **Ask for clarification/explanation if you hear jargon, slang or acronyms that you don't recognize.** This can happen while you're presenting to an international audience (from the US, for example). People may be so used to the way they speak normally at work with their colleagues and even though they are aware that you are from a different country, they may talk to you or ask you questions in the same way they speak to their colleagues. So they speak American English business jargon or use acronyms that you're not familiar with. The way to handle this is to not get flustered or look intimidated, but to politely and clearly let them know that you don't understand and ask then to explain. For example, a common English phrase we use in the US is "I'm between a rock and a hard place", which means that I'm in a tough situation where neither of my choices or decisions is ideal and both have undesirable impacts. Don't be shy – ask for explanation.

- **Use of graphics or visual aids.** This is a good way to make your presentation easier to understand and get your point across. For example, when my team presented to a Chinese audience about our new computer, we would have the actual computer in the room. We opened the computer casing to show the key sections and components inside. The team used the computer as a visual aid to demonstrate their key points and it was also an effective technique to get the audience engaged. While your customers may not feel comfortable asking questions in the room, they can inspect the product first-hand and get many of their questions answered.

- **Offer one-on-one meetings after the presentation.** Because the audience may not feel comfortable asking questions publicly, they may welcome a chance to speak to you one-on-one. This is very common in Asia and almost a must have. If possible, time and space should be set aside for these follow-on interactions. Remember to allocate time after your presentation and invite them to talk with you and discuss any questions they may have.

COMMUNICATING AND PRESENTING TO A LARGE AUDIENCE

With a larger audience size, presentations must have an even more focused and clear story line. As a volunteer for the Red Cross training academy, I often present and teach humanitarian subjects. To connect with the audience and highlight the relevance of the context, I have often used the Korean drama, "Descendants of the Sun". In all cases, it immediately connected with the audience as the majority of Asians can relate to the story lines and characters. In addition, during the presentation, scan the audience for supporters that you can call on to share their insights. It serves as reinforcement of ideas for the audience.

COMMUNICATING AND PRESENTING SPONTANEOUSLY

With more and more companies having a flat organization structure, employees are more likely to engage top management in hallway conversations or water-cooler chats. Such situations could take the place of some formal meetings. With so much information overloading the executives, it's essential to have the ability to engage in productive and brief conversations (3–5 minutes). While this activity may not be natural to all of us, I would recommend that you practise conversing in this kind of situation as it is increasingly an important skillset professionally as well as socially.

Three characteristics of such spontaneous situations:

- Listen and recognize the broader conversation setting so you can align your topic to it. Whether it's a business meeting or trade conference, you should seize the opportunity and prepare potential topical content for exchanging ideas thoughtfully and engaging in relevant dialogues.

- Be flexible to the meeting format. The key objective is to convey your main theme, ideas, and passion to the target audience in a succinct way.

- Be able to summarize. To convey a lot of information in a few minutes, being able to summarize is a key skill to practise. Structure the dialogue by summarizing the top ideas, then the follow-on actions for impact and benefits, as well as briefly covering important background information.

Successful Meetings

Pre-meeting: Structure it right

- Clear objective
- Only invite those who matter
- Agenda planning
- Reasonable time slots

Managing the meeting

- Start on time
- Reiterate meeting objective
- Drive closure on topics
- Time management – start/end each agenda item on time
- Manage the flow, encourage participation
- Don't be sidetracked by irrelevant discussions
- End meeting on time
- Summarise outcomes
- Document key agreements
- Create follow-up actions

Post-meeting: Follow up tight

- Follow-up meetings
- Progress to next checkpoint meeting
- Continuation to close unfinished topics
- Offline meetings for spin-off discussions
- Track action item completions

How to Run and Facilitate Meetings

One of the most precious commodities we have is time. We value time. We usually feel we don't have enough time to get things done. This is especially true at work. We are rushing against deadlines and wishing we had more time to do a more thorough job. One of the most time-consuming activities at work is attending meetings. There are many types of meeting: company meetings, staff meetings, project team meetings, one-on-one meetings with your manager or co-workers, meetings with customers and external parties, meetings to address unexpected crises or urgent issues, impromptu meetings, etc.

The majority of meetings are run inefficiently. They take longer than needed, and oftentimes, little gets accomplished, or worse yet, confusion arises and as a result, another meeting has to be called to revisit the issue. This wastes time and frustrates people who could have used the time more productively. One main reason for inefficiently run meetings is the lack of know-how from the meeting facilitator.

You will have opportunities to run meetings in your career. Knowing how to do so effectively will save you and your co-workers valuable time and foster a positive working environment. In this chapter, I will cover the best ways to run an effective meeting and achieve the meeting's goals.

HOW TO PREPARE FOR THE MEETING

- **Understand the meeting's goal clearly.** Is it an informational meeting where people share knowledge, a meeting to review project status and progress, a meeting to discuss and solve a problem, or a meeting to reach a decision? This helps you determine the right people to attend the meeting, set the agenda, determine the length of the meeting and ensure people are prepared.

- **Determine the meeting's attendees.** For the meeting to be effective and productive, only people who are needed should attend. Very often, a meeting has too many people, including some who don't add any value. If these people like to talk, they can dominate the meeting and run the risk of ending it without accomplishing what you wanted. When you put the list of attendees together, ask yourself what each of their roles are, what value they add, and what the impact would be without their participation. This is especially important for working meetings where the team needs to make decisions, solve a problem or review project progress. When you schedule a meeting and send out the agenda, include a note to let meeting participants know to check with you if they would like to invite anyone else. You are the meeting facilitator and you have the final say on the attendees.

- **Have a clear agenda.** When you schedule the meeting and send out the invites, include a short but clear message stating:

  ▷ Purpose of the meeting. For example: "Purpose of meeting is to finalize the project proposal to be sent to CEO Executive staff for approval" or "Purpose of the meeting is to finalize the XYZ project schedule."

  ▷ Agenda items. List out the items you plan to cover with the team during the meeting. List the name of each person responsible for covering a specific item. Allocate the amount of time for each item so the item's owner knows how to prepare. For example, if the meeting is to finalize the project schedule, your agenda could be as follows:

    • Product requirements – John S (15 minutes)
    • Design requirements – Betty J (15 minutes)
    • Quality plan – Manish T (15 minutes)
    • Manufacturing plan – Tom R (15 minutes)

  ▷ Ask anyone who has suggestions on the agenda to contact you before the meeting. Also ask the item owners to let you know if they will not be ready so you can revise the agenda accordingly.

▷ Include the meeting location in your invite if possible. If you have people who will be attending on the phone or via video-conferencing, make sure the meeting room has the IT equipment you need. Many meetings start late due to people scrambling to find out where the meeting is or missing the IT equipment needed for the meeting.

HOW TO MANAGE THE MEETING

• Start on time. It is common to be late to events or meetings. However, in conducting business, especially with American colleagues, customers or partners and others in the Western world, punctuality is not only important, but is a judgment on a person's credibility. We are creatures of habit. If you set a hard start time and stick to it, eventually people will get the message and be at the meeting on time. You may want to allocate five minutes at the beginning of the meeting to allow people leaving from a previous meeting to get to your meeting. But do not let five minutes become ten. Remember, you probably won't have the luxury to make up for lost time.

• Start the meeting by reiterating the purpose of the meeting and reviewing the agenda to make sure everyone is on the same page. If someone wants to modify the meeting or add to the meeting, you need to make a judgment call on whether their request is appropriate for the meeting and can be accommodated within the meeting's time. Normally, I would recommend no. That person should have added it to the agenda prior to the meeting. If the request is important enough to the meeting's objectives and the person is ready to cover the new item, you may add it to the agenda. Otherwise, ask that person to work offline with you.

- Monitor the progress of the agenda to make sure each item has the allocated time. If the discussion on a particular item is taking longer, you can check with the team to see if the remaining agenda items would take less time and allow this person to continue. Or you can ask them to wrap up and continue offline after the meeting. If someone asks a question that's not relevant to the topic, remind that person of the topic being discussed and ask to discuss it after the meeting. For example: "Sorry Pat, we are tight on time and we're discussing topic ABC. Can you discuss that offline after the meeting?"

- Confirm the outcome of each major agenda item. For the example above, when a team member finishes his product requirement discussion and agrees to a timeline, capture the results and confirm with him.

- If a conflict or debate occurs, let the discussion happen within the time allowed. However, make sure people don't talk over each other and each person is heard. If everyone is talking at the same time, you can interject firmly to remind people that one person should speak at a time. Make sure the discussion is focusing on the work issue and not personal. If someone is getting emotional and attacking someone personally, you need to intervene immediately and emphasize the need to focus on the issue. Cut off that discussion and continue with the meeting's topic. You need to take control of the meeting.

- Monitor to see if discussions are related to the agenda topic. If a discussion is getting off track, stop the discussion and bring it back to the meeting's agenda. For example: "We are tight on time and need to focus on our agenda to finish our meeting. So let's get back on track."

- Before ending the meeting, summarize and verbalize the outcomes and next steps to all the meeting participants to make sure all attendees, especially people on the phone, are on the same page. If some team members have a different understanding, they have a chance to raise the issue and resolve it right away. And if some participants seem confused or disagree with the summary, discuss the issue right away and either come up with an agreement, a solution or at least the next step to resolve this issue. Don't leave the meeting with the issue in limbo. As soon as you can after the meeting, send out the meeting summary so everyone can refer back to if there's any question in the future. This will save you a lot of time from revisiting the meeting outcomes again.

- If you conduct the meeting with other attendees who are fluent in English or English is their native language while it's not yours, you need to make sure they understand what you're saying and as importantly, you need to understand them. If you are speaking, ask them if they have any questions or want more explanation from you. Remember to speak clearly and loud enough (don't mumble). If they ask you a question that you're not sure you understand, ask them to clarify. Likewise, if some attendees speak, ask them to repeat or explain if you're confused or don't clearly understand. When you conduct the meeting in English and you have people from different ethnic backgrounds attending for whom English is not their native language, be respectful to their needs. Remember to speak clearly and frequently check with them to make sure they understand what you're saying. Remind others in the meeting to speak clearly too.

- Using humour is a good technique to enhance the working environment, defuse tensions and promote teamwork. So be yourself and use your sense of humour at appropriate times in the meeting. However, be sensitive to people's feelings and don't offend them with dark humour or insensitive jokes, such as jokes about people's race, sex, physical appearance, etc.

COMMON MISTAKES IN FACILITATING MEETINGS

- Too many people in the meeting. As a general rule, the larger the meeting, the less you will be able to get things done. If you have a meeting with too many people, determine who is really needed and disinvite people who are not. How many is too many depends on the context of your meeting. If it is a working or decision-making meeting, I believe less than ten is more conducive to having a productive meeting. If it is an informational meeting where no deep discussion or decision is required, a larger number of people can attend.

- Not keeping the meeting on track to be able to cover all the agenda items adequately, potentially result-ing in sub-optimal results and rushed decisions. If you have to schedule another meeting because you weren't able to cover all the topics, you're taking more time out of your and other people's schedules. If you need to focus on facilitating the meeting and are not able to monitor the time, ask one of the participants to be a timekeeper for you.

- Failure to summarize key points, decisions, action items and next steps from the meeting. Forgetting or ignoring this important step can cause confusion or miscommunication. People are usually multi-tasking and probably don't remember all the details from the many meetings they attended. Having a written summary that team members can refer to will help save headaches and precious time.

- Failure to get full participation from the meeting participants. This is especially common when you have meetings with both people attending in person and people attending virtually. Keep a list of the virtual attendees and remember to repeat key discussion points and confirm their understanding. Also remember to check if they have questions or comments.

- Too many conversations are happening at the same time. If you facilitate a meeting from a remote location and the attendees are either on the phone or gathered in a conference room, the above practices are also relevant. However, since you are remote, you need to be more assertive in running the meeting. Listen for side conversations and put a stop to them; they are distracting to the meeting agenda. If multiple people are talking and making it difficult to hear, intervene right away. In addition, do your best to have video systems setup to enable people to see the meeting materials.

International companies with Western culture place a lot of emphasis on time efficiency. This counters many Asian markets that have flexible time handling approach. Develop excellent time management and meeting efficiency skills will set you up well within a multinational company environment.

Collaborate Successfully

Skills and qualities
- Adaptability
- Communication skills
- Negotiation skills

Strategies

Setup for good start
- Clarify goals to focus everyone
- Align clear understanding of deliverables and timeline
- Clarify individual tasks, responsibility, deliverables, deadlines
- Understand dependencies
- Team working model

Clear documentation
- Project manager to send post-meeting summary
- Central information bank

Leadership
- Lead by example
- Assist team members
- Identify problems early
- Focus on business issues
- Compliment/reward members
- Celebrate milestones

Communications
- Seek and give regular feedback
- Update managers on progress

Conflict resolution
- Deal with issues early
- Don't make things personal
- Identify root causes
- Brainstorm solutions
- Escalate for help if necessary

How to Collaborate Successfully

Collaboration means to work jointly with someone or a group of people on an activity, especially to create or produce something. Regardless of your profession, it's rare when you work alone. You spend most of your time working with people in your company as well as external parties, including customers, suppliers, partners and consultants. These people play a key role in determining how successful you will be. In this chapter, I'll explain the importance of having good collaboration skills, the skills and qualities you need to be a good collaborator, as well as strategies and techniques you can develop and use in different working situations.

WHY HAVING GOOD COLLABORATION SKILLS IS IMPORTANT

Before we delve into the strategies, let's first understand the benefits of being a good collaborator.

- You normally spend a lot of time working with other people on a team project. Everybody needs to do their part and deliver on their commitment in order for the whole project to be successful. Because a project is only going to be as strong as the weakest link in the chain, team members are dependent on each other and need to work together closely. Collaborating effectively is the key to a successful project.

- Effective collaboration enables you and the team to work more efficiently. Teams who don't collaborate well often have miscommunication, confusion and conflict – all of which result in loss of critical time. For example, I have been on teams where we had multiple meetings rehashing the same topic, revisiting decisions or clarifying unnecessary confusion. Teams that work well together only meet as needed and use meetings to set goals, review project status and resolve issues. If you have good collaboration skills and use them to help your team work effectively together, you not only help your team but also yourself by saving time to work on other important activities.

- How you perform on a project and how you work with other people is a major factor on your performance review. Your team members and other managers' feedback have significant influence on how you will be evaluated. Positive feedback along with delivering excellent results will earn you good performance reviews, salary raises and consideration for promotions. I consistently noticed during my career that high performers share one common trait: the ability to work with people to get things done successfully.

- In collaborating with people, whether in a leading role or as a team member, you have a great opportunity to grow professionally, develop leadership skills, enhance communication skills and improve your ability to work effectively with others. Moreover, demonstrating good collaboration skills is a great way to make you stand out at work and get the attention of company executives.

- In today's professional working environment, oftentimes you'll work with people outside of your company, including customers, suppliers, partners and even your competitors. Your customers and partners especially can have different priorities from your company or they feel they have an advantage over you and, as a result, may make unreasonable demands on you and your company. In these situations, striving to achieve win-win outcomes is important and this will require great collaboration and negotiation skills.

Companies spend a significant amount of money to train their employees on teamwork. I once had an employee, Mark, who was an expert in his field, knew his stuff inside out but was not good at working with people and getting people to do what he needed to complete the project. If Mark could develop and improve this skillset, he would be a star. I sent him to a one-week professional development training programme at the cost of $5,000, not including hotel, travel and food expenses. This not only cost the company a lot of money, but more importantly, five days of productive work from him. If you had or developed these skills early in your career, you will have a leg up in your career and a great head-start over other people.

Let me explain how to effectively collaborate with other people and get them to collaborate with you.

SKILLS AND QUALITIES NEEDED FOR EFFECTIVE COLLABORATION

I'll discuss three important skills and qualities: adaptability, communication and negotiation.

- **Adaptability.** People you work with may come from different cultures, different backgrounds, have different personalities and working styles. Since there is no "one size fits all" approach to working with others and getting the most out of their effort, you need to be able to adapt to them. Invest your time on your team members to develop a rapport and understand how best to work with them – what motivates them, what work methods they prefer, what makes them tick, etc. Investing this time will go a long way in gaining their trust and set you up to work well with them.

- **Communication skills.** Having good communication skills goes hand in hand with collaboration skills.

I covered this in detail in the "How to communicate effectively" chapter. Specifically, I talked about the importance of being a good listener. Moreover, I covered ways to communicate in different work situations. Lastly, I discussed the importance of maintaining professionalism, staying focused on the business issue and not reacting personally in difficult situations.

- **Negotiation skills.** This is the ability to influence people to achieve a mutually desired outcome. Even without being aware of it, we frequently negotiate. We negotiate with our manager on work assignments and priorities, with team members on project tasks and deadlines, with suppliers on material cost and delivery schedule, etc. Negotiating with other people plays a key role in collaboration. Refer to my other book in this series, *Powerful Work Hacks*, for details. I describe a strategy and approach to use in any negotiation, the need to gather as much information as possible, to be creative, and most importantly, to achieve a win-win outcome.

COLLABORATION STRATEGIES

Try these strategies for collaborating effectively on a team project.

- This is more applicable to the project manager, but even if you are not, you can play an active role in spending time in the beginning of a project to:

▷ Clarify the goals/objectives to make sure everyone is on the same page. If there is any confusion, this is the time to clarify and confirm project goals and objectives. If and when issues arise causing the project to get off track, going back to the project objectives is a good way to refocus everyone.

▷ Discuss and gain clear understanding of deliverables and timelines expected of the team. Moreover, it's important to align with management on the deliverables since they will hold the team accountable to these commitments. If the team cannot commit to the expected deliverables and timelines, they must negotiate with the management team.

▷ Clarify your specific tasks/responsibilities, negotiate and prioritize your deliverables and deadlines. Be thorough in assessing your tasks and schedules before committing. While you want to be aggressive, try not to over-commit to action items you don't have control over or confidence to deliver on time. All things being equal, it's better to under-promise and over-deliver.

▷ Understand your dependencies on other people and vice versa. Know specifically whom you need to work with to make sure they deliver to you what you need to complete your job.

▷ Determine how team members prefer to work together – method of communication, frequency of meetings, forums to resolve issues/conflicts, etc.

- Spend time to figure out effective ways to work with your team members as discussed in the "Adaptability" paragraph earlier.

- At the end of each meeting, make sure there is a meeting recap that summarizes decisions made, action items/owners and next steps. This helps eliminate confusion among team members and prevent wasting time from needing another meeting to clear things up. Confusion can easily happen when many topics are discussed at the meeting. To ensure team members are on the same page, the project manager should send out a summary message after the meeting.

- Create a central online shared workspace for sharing information, work in progress, and capturing up-to-date changes and status. This enables everyone to see the same work being done as well as changes made in real time and ensures everyone has the same information at all times. There are many online workspace tools available. Check with your company's IT group.

- Lead by example. Meeting your commitments and completing your deliverables on time gains you credibility and trust from team members. Moreover, looking for opportunities to put the team above individual results is a good way to show your leadership skills. For example, offer your team members a hand when they need help.

- Identify problems/conflicts early and resolve them as soon as possible. Refer to the "How to handle conflicts and difficult situations" chapter for ways to handle these situations. Focus on the business issue and not on personal matters.

- Seek regular feedback from team members and give constructive feedback as appropriate. This enables any confusion between team members to get cleared up and gives everyone the opportunity to make improvements on their work.

- Keep your manager updated on the project status and your progress. This enables your manager to keep the upper management team up to date and allows you to seek help if and when you need it.

- Know when to escalate for help. You need to use your judgment here. While we may want to try to solve problems ourselves, sometimes we need help. It's always better to ask for help than to miss your deadline. Your manager would much prefer to have you ask for help than hear the bad news about the project. Your boss' obvious question then would be: "Why didn't you ask for help sooner?"

- Compliment and reward people for excellent work and teamwork effort. People appreciate being recognized for their work, so even a small gesture of sending an email to thank them for their effort and copying their manager goes a long way in building strong team spirit.

- Celebrate key milestones and accomplishments. Many of us put our heads down to finish our work and then move on to the next project without taking time to celebrate the team's accomplishments. It's an opportunity to catch our breath, enjoy each other's company and recognize our own contribution to the success of the project. Moreover, it offers a great way to gain visibility and recognition.

RESOLVING CONFLICTS AND CHALLENGES

Inevitably, there will be conflicts or issues that arise during a project. The team's ability to stay on track and complete the project on time depends on the team members' ability to address and resolve these issues in a timely and productive fashion. Here is a summary of the steps to follow when a conflict arises:

- Recognize the issue early. Don't ignore and hope it will go away.

- Focus on the work issue and not personal issues.

- Identify the root causes of the issue – be honest and objective.

- Once root causes are identified, hold frank discussion to brainstorm potential solutions.

- Decide which solution is best to implement. If need be, escalate to management for help.

Let's take an example. A team member is not meeting his commitment and that is impacting your work. Because your specific project deliverables are dependent on his deliverables, you cannot perform your work without his output. As a result, the team risks not meeting the deadline. You are in a bind. What should you do?

- Seek to understand the root cause. Talk to this team member to understand why he's not able to complete his work and help him understand that this is impacting the entire team's project. Don't make any assumption about why he is not delivering on his commitment and avoid making any accusations. Maintain your professionalism and focus on the business issue.

- Once you understand why, offer to brainstorm with him ways to help him complete his work so you will be able to do your work and the project can get back on track. Let's assume that he was late because he had to take time off to attend to a family matter. Knowing this was the reason and not his competence or motivation, you can offer to take on some part of his work so both of you will be able to catch up. This will earn you good-will and trust that will be helpful in future projects. If you found out he was just lazy and not motivated to do his work or if he rejects your offer to help, you should escalate the matter to the project manager to help resolve the issue. Before escalating, let him know the step you plan to take. While he may not like this, he should understand you have tried your best to resolve the issue with him, but you must put the team first.

THINK WIN-WIN IN COLLABORATION

It's essential in a collaboration approach to avoid "zero-sum game" situations. Such thoughts would place the parties into competing mode. Alignment on common ground is an important early step to establish rationale for shared goals or gains. For example, instead of just thinking as competing soccer teams, a common vision of the competing teams coming together to create a championship league which would increase the fan base would be an example of win-win thinking in a competitive environment.

In the case of international collaboration (usually from the company's worldwide HQ with local Asian markets), it's important to know your value-add in the entire value chain. For example, your local market knowledge and access gives you credibility and a good starting point in the collaboration effort. In addition, smaller markets in Asia give us insight of the process end-to-end vis-à-vis larger homogeneous markets such as the US.

While I have covered collaborating in the context of a team project, many of these strategies and techniques also apply to other situations, including working one-on-one with people in other functions and third parties.

How to Get People to Listen

One question I frequently get from my students, employees and co-workers is: "How do I get people to listen to me?" Particularly in meetings, people have things to say and they get impatient when other people talk too much. They in turn may react by interrupting and speaking louder, resulting in a lot of people talking over each other and nobody really listens. Moreover, when in a large group meeting, we feel hesitant to speak up for fear of saying dumb things and embarrassing ourselves. We keep quiet while wishing we could speak up and get people to pay attention. I'll cover in this chapter the qualities needed and the best ways to get people to listen to you, especially in a group meeting setting. Many Asians need an extra push to speak freely. This chapter is critical for bringing your ability to an international level.

Here are the qualities needed to get people's attention.

- **Build credibility with the people you work with.** This doesn't happen on day one. This is something we earn over time. Credibility is earned by meeting our commitments, delivering results on time, being dependable, and helping out when needed. In

Get People to Listen

Getting attention in meetings

- Understand the context of the meeting
- Prepare and act accordingly
- Listen, seek to understand
- Build rapport
- Seek opportunities to offer comment
  - *Make it a habit to speak up, and prepare potential comments*
- Know when to interject
- Express disagreement professionally
- Don't take negative comments personally
- Be comfortable speaking up:
  - Speak loud and clear
  - Establish eye contact
  - Practise for confidence

Qualities needed

- Build credibility with people you work with
- Earn trust with respect
- Be a good listener

addition, if you could develop a specific standout skill and use it to help people, you will go a long way in building credibility.

- **Earn trust by treating people with respect.** When you are a good team player who shows genuine care for your co-workers, they will tend to give you the benefit of the doubt because they believe you are honest and put the interest of the team ahead of your own. Respect what people say and genuinely seek to understand instead of being condescending or abrupt. People in turn will reciprocate that respect. When you speak up, people will listen, take your words at face value and not have to wonder if you have any hidden agenda.

- **Being a good listener.** This is a key part of communication skill. When we listen to people carefully, we understand their issues better and that helps us respond more appropriately. Moreover, it will encourage them to be more open to what you say. A good communicator is also an excellent listener. If you are new to the meeting and don't know people there, asking questions and listening to them is a good way to establish rapport.

HOW TO GET PEOPLE'S ATTENTION IN MEETINGS

I'll focus on a group meeting setting for this discussion.

- **Understand the context of the meeting.** Is it a meeting where you're there to receive information, review a project's progress, solve a problem or reach a recommendation for management? Knowing the context of the meeting will help you prepare appropriately and identify ways you can contribute. If it's an informational meeting, you can participate by asking for clarification, praising the value of the information received and suggesting additional information needed. If it's a project status meeting, be prepared to review your own work progress, answer questions people may have and discuss your team members' work. If it's a meeting to address and solve a problem, you can play a mediator role to keep people on track, focus on the issue at hand and to offer potential ideas for people to consider.

- **Listen and pay attention to people's comments.** Before you speak, focus on listening to what people are saying. Is it clear to you? If not, ask them to clarify. Something like: "Could you clarify that for me. I just want to make sure I understand your points clearly." And if you want to respond or add to their comment, say: "What you're saying about XYZ is really helpful, and I would like to add to that."

- **Build rapport.** Ask for clarifications or rephrase their comment to avoid misunderstanding. This is a good way to connect with people and to show you are interested and engaged in their work. This will also help people feel more comfortable engaging with you. If you are new to the project and fear that you may ask a dumb question, you can preface your question by saying: "I'm new to this and sorry if this is redundant, but I was wondering if you could elaborate on that point for me."

- **Seek opportunities to offer comments.** Once you know the purpose of the meeting and have prepared yourself, look for opportunities to chime in. Keep in mind that having well-thought-out comments will give you credibility and the confidence to speak up. As you listen to someone in the meeting and decide you want to respond, wait until that person finishes his thought. Acknowledge his point and offer your own comments. For example: "That's a really good point, John. I would also like to add to that..." or if you're having a hard time chiming in, raise your hand clearly for people to see and firmly state: "I'm hearing a lot of good points and I also have a couple of comments I would like to share with you."

- **Know when to interject.** If you are in a contentious meeting where people are speaking over one another, it's fruitless for you to interject with your comments. At some point, the meeting facilitator should step in and take control of the meeting. Then you can take advantage of this opportunity to raise your hand and say: "I have a comment I would like to add." Then proceed with your comment. If the facilitator is not taking control of the meeting, wait for a good time to interrupt with a friendly but firm voice: "We're not making progress here when everyone is speaking at once. Let's have one person speaking at a time." Then gesture to the meeting facilitator to resume running the meeting. A simple gesture like that shows your assertiveness and also demonstrates your leadership quality.

- **Express your disagreement professionally.** Base your comments on the issue and not the person by focusing on what they do and not who they are. For example: "I believe your plan is missing some key details" as opposed to "You are clueless." Acknowledge their points before you express your opinions. For example: "I understand and appreciate your points and perspective, but I see the issue differently. Here's why...." When you're finished, you can ask for feedback: "Is it clear what I said? Any questions or anything you want me to elaborate on?"

- **Remember to speak up.** It's to your benefit to speak up in the meeting. If you don't, nobody knows who you are and what value you add. If you don't think you have any valid points to add, ask someone to elaborate on their points. At least this will allow people to see you, hear you and it helps you feel more comfortable speaking up later. Make a habit of speaking in a meeting at least twice, especially when you're in a meeting with your boss or company executives. This is your opportunity to be recognized, get visibility and to make a good impression with the management team. Thinking ahead of time about potential comments and insight that would be good to bring up in the meeting will make it easier for you to speak up.

- **Don't take people's criticism or negative comments personally.** Ask for clarification or specific details. Even when someone gets personal with you and makes condescending remarks, resist the urge to lash back. Put the ball back in that person's court by making them focus on the topic and the facts. For example, if Ted comments, "You don't make any sense with your analysis," you should reply with: "Ted, can you give me the specifics on the part of my analysis that didn't make sense to you." This puts the onus on Ted to give examples or risk looking bad with the people in the room.

- **Can you hear me?** When speaking, make sure you speak in a clear and loud enough voice for everyone to hear. In addition, look at the people you are talking to. This shows you are engaging actively and expressing your views confidently. Try to minimize word fillers such as "um" and "ah". They can make you appear timid and lacking conviction in your comments. If you have this habit, practise in a safe environment with friendly people you're comfortable with. If you are nervous, take deep breaths. With practice and repetition, you will be more comfortable speaking up. Especially if English is not your native language, you need to focus even more on speaking clearly and making sure people understand you. Make a habit of asking them if they have any questions or want you to elaborate on what you were saying.

How to Give and Receive Feedback

Giving and receiving feedback is a regular practice in the corporate world, especially in Western business environments. Formal feedback takes place at annual or semi-annual employee performance reviews. This is when your manager solicits feedback from people you worked with throughout the year – your team members, co-workers, project managers, managers as well as people outside the company. Their feedback plays a significant role in how you will be evaluated. Delivering good results is only one part of your evaluation. How you work with other people is just as important.

As a manager, I was often puzzled when someone on my team expressed surprise at the feedback from their peers. If you have an open communication channel with people in the company and you pay attention to your working relationship with them, you shouldn't be surprised at the feedback you receive. Moreover, it shouldn't be that the first time you hear feedback is at your formal performance review. You should be asking for feedback from the people you work with and from your manager on a regular basis; this helps you address any issues that may exist, gives

Mindset reframe

- Feedback is not criticism
- Regular formal feedback
- Poor feedback could be improved

Give and Receive Feedback

Giving feedback

- Give feedback on specifics
- Appropriate time and space
- Right state of mind
- Prepare constructive message
- Listen

Receiving feedback

- Be proactive in seeking regular input
- Listen calmly, don't be defensive
- Reflect with open mind
- Validate the specifics
- Take corrective actions if feedback is valid
- Get back to show feedback taken seriously

you a chance to clarify and take corrective actions when things are still fresh for both sides. In addition, if you are able to resolve these issues in a timely way, chances are these issues will not reflect negatively on you when your peers give their feedback for your formal performance review. Better yet, they will more likely appreciate your proactive effort to reach out and improve your working relationships with them.

Other managers will also ask you to give feedback on their employees who have worked with you over the past year. Well before the employee evaluation meeting, I would ask for feedback on each of my employees from people who have worked with them. Knowing how to receive and give feedback is an important skill. The good news is this skill is not difficult to learn. In this chapter, I'll share the best ways you can use to receive and give feedback, and have this skill as another tool in your toolbox.

Giving and receiving feedback is important for several reasons:

- Helps your team members be better at their jobs. We all want to improve our job performance and any help we can get to help us achieve this would be welcome.

- A good practice to build and maintain relationships if giving and receiving feedback is done the right way.

- Effective way to ensure you and others are on the same page. Any conflicts are brought up and addressed promptly.

- An excellent way to recognize someone for their good work as well as an opportunity to influence and persuade them.

- A great practice for you to continue to develop your interpersonal and communication skill.

Many of us view feedback as unpleasant and associate it with criticism. However, it should be seen as a positive communication vehicle. Simply put, feedback is not criticism. Criticism is being negative, and it comes across as judgmental and even personal. Moreover, it tends to make the person on the receiving end defensive and as a result, inhibits productive discussion. Feedback, on the other hand, is positive communication with good intentions. It's constructive and collaborative. It's intended to recognize others for their good work and help them improve their performance.

HOW TO GIVE FEEDBACK SUCCESSFULLY

Follow these steps to help you prepare and give feedback constructively.

- **Think about what you want to give feedback on.** What were the specific issues that triggered your desire to give feedback? Is there anything you need to clarify? Do you need to check with anyone else to validate the issues? The more specific the issues, the more effective you will be able to give feedback.

- **Pick an appropriate place and time to meet.** When you want to give someone feedback, it's best to have the conversation between just the two of you. This promotes an open environment for dialogue, especially if you don't know how sensitive the other person will be. You want to avoid any risk of embarrassing them in front of other people, even if that was not at all your intention. In addition, be aware of their mood and state of mind before you start. If they seem under a lot of stress, unhappy or on a tight work deadline, wait for another time. If you're not sure, check if this is a good time to talk: "Kelly, is this a good time to talk? I was wondering if I could have a few minutes to share some feedback with you."

- **Prepare your message.** The message should be constructive, not critical. Stay on the issue, on what that person did and not who they are. Bring specific examples to clarify your points. For example: "Tom, I've been thinking about your recent report on the team project. The report made some really good points. I also have some ideas and feedback to help make the report even stronger. Would it be okay for us to discuss them?" This focuses on the report Tom wrote and nothing about him personally. Of course, any smart person would accept your invitation to offer ideas and feedback. Contrast that comment with: "Tom, I don't know what you were thinking when you wrote that report. It makes no sense. You have a lot of work to do to fix it. I have some ideas." This is derogatory and insulting since it implies Tom is stupid. Starting with this comment will not likely result in a good, productive discussion.

- **Listen.** A key part of giving feedback is listening to the other person. Allow them time to reflect on your feedback and to respond. Ask them if what you said was clear or if they need you to clarify. Listen carefully to their response. Don't get defensive if they're not taking what you said seriously. Don't get rattled if they take it personally and react emotionally. Try to understand their reaction. Ask: "I'm sorry you seem upset. Was there something specific about my feedback that made you feel this way?" Then listen. Affirm with them that your only objective is to be constructive and to help. Before you end the discussion, ask them for their opinions on the way you gave feedback and how you can give feedback better next time.

- **Know the person you want to give feedback to.** While the steps I mentioned above are very effective in giving feedback, it's good to take into account the person you're giving feedback to may have a different personality, background or come from a different region/country with a different culture from yours. They may interpret what you say differently from what you meant or react to your feedback in unexpected ways. Therefore, it's to your benefit to get to know your colleagues (as I mentioned in the "How to earn trust" chapter), so you can be prepared in giving your feedback. And if you have their trust, they would take your feedback more seriously.

HOW TO GIVE AND RECEIVE FEEDBACK

This skill will stand you in good stead if and when you become a manager. One of the responsibilities managers have is to coach their employees, which involves giving feedback. Your employees will want and expect to get feedback from you on a regular basis.

HOW TO RECEIVE FEEDBACK

In addition to willingly sitting down with your co-workers to receive their feedback, it's even better to proactively seek them out. This shows you are taking the initiative to continue to get better. It puts people at ease knowing that you welcome and look forward to their feedback. By asking them, you let them know you give them the green light to be frank, you value their feedback and you want to build a good working relationship with them. Here are some of the best practices for you.

- **Listen.** If you initiate the conversation, let them know at the beginning of the meeting that you appreciate their time and you value their feedback. You especially look forward to receiving constructive and productive feedback to help you improve. Also be specific about what issue you are asking for feedback on. Is it about a recent presentation you delivered or an analysis you recently completed? Is it about your participation or interaction with the team members of the project? Is it about how you handled a recent conflict?

  Whether you asked for or agreed to receive feedback, the first and foremost important thing is to listen. Listen carefully to what they say. Try not to get defensive. Repeat their comment to make sure you understood. For example: "What I hear you say is that my presentation was good but was missing supporting data. Did I hear you correctly?" Or ask them to clarify if you are unclear about their comment: "I just want to make sure I understand what you said. Can you elaborate on your comments for me?" Make a note of the feedback so you can reflect on it at a later time. This is especially useful for critical feedback because we may get defensive when we first hear the feedback and not consider it objectively.

If you feel they are being personal and criticizing you, stay calm and try not to take it personally. Instead, ask them for specific examples. This will confirm if they are being constructive or just wanting to give you a hard time. For example: "How is what you just said related to what I did? Can you help me understand?" Or: "Julie, I'm not sure I understood clearly. Could you give me a specific example of what I did?" If Julie is still vague and making general comments, suggest that she come back with some examples: "Julie, it would help me if you could think of a specific example. We can get together later when you're ready." Now the ball is in her court.

- **What to do with the feedback you received.** First of all, with an open mind, reflect and consider the feedback. Was it constructive? Was it valid? Was it specific enough? Did you agree with it? Was it something you can act on? If there were other people involved and they have knowledge of the situation, you can also cross-check with them. You don't need to reveal the identity of the person giving you the feedback. You can mention that you recently received some feedback and wanted to validate it with them. For example: "John, I received some feedback on my presentation in our meeting a couple of days ago and I would love to run it by you to get your thoughts. I want to make my presentation better and your feedback would be great. Would that be okay?" Then describe the feedback and listen for his response.

Next, decide what you would like to do with the feedback. Do you think it was valid and want to make corrections or implement their suggestions? Or do you decide to do nothing because the feedback did not have validity? If you decide to take actions based on their feedback, take an opportunity to get back to that person and let them know. They would appreciate your taking their feedback seriously.

- **Make it a habit to seek regular feedback as appropriate.** Your manager is an excellent person to give you feedback. Seek opportunities after a key project is completed, when a key milestone is achieved or after your presentation that your manager attended. If important stakeholders will read your written report, ask your manager to review it first. If you seek feedback regularly and take positive actions, you increase your chances of getting a good performance review because you will be able to demonstrate your effectiveness and success in working with people. Moreover, you are less likely to be caught blindsided during your performance review.

- **Mentor/reverse mentor.** From my experience, it is very beneficial to invest in such partnerships. Once you have such an arrangement, it would be much more natural to have conversations. This kind of relationship also provides a safe environment to practise feedback techniques and expand the scope of topics. With increased comfort level, individual personal pride and concerns no longer present a challenge to engaging with our partners.

How to Handle Conflicts and Difficult Situations

When I joined an aerospace company as a new engineering graduate, I encountered a volatile situation at work during my very first project. Each of the software engineers on the team, which was tasked with delivering a test program for a fighter aircraft, owned a specific software module of the overall program. In order for the program to work properly, all the modules had to integrate seamlessly and work flawlessly together. When I and another senior programmer – Jim, who had been working at the company for several years – tried to integrate our respective modules, they failed to work. This was a bit of a disaster since other team members couldn't move forward without our successful integration. When this failure occurred, Jim's face turned red and he began yelling at me, blaming me for the failure and saying my program was a piece of "crap" (he used a more colourful word).

Throughout your career, you will face difficult situations –work conflicts, unexpected events or surprises that will test your ability to stay calm, hold your poise under pressure and think

Handle Difficult Situations

Common approach
- Professionalism
- Focus on listening to understand
- Prepare in-depth
- Define problem clearly; logical approach

Dealing with

Difficult customer
- Listen and understand the problems
- Own the problem for the company
- Potential turn around with resolution
- Treat customer engagement for better understanding

Conflict with co-workers
- Stay calm; don't get emotional
- Clarify and understand the issues
- Focus on issue resolution

Conflict with boss
- Learn to say no smartly

Situation with executives
- Anticipate executive-level questions
- Clarify questions, definitions, assumptions
- Buy time to respond
- Handle questions/objections professionally

Last-minute surprises
- Expect the unexpected
- Plan for contingencies

on your feet. These situations could arise from any number of circumstances, from dealing with co-workers and company management to managing external parties, including customers, partners and suppliers.

While it is impossible to anticipate and prepare for every situation, there is a basic approach you can apply to most situations. In this chapter, I'll discuss the general best practices and behaviour we should utilize when facing a challenging situation. In addition, I'll cover some specific scenarios, their unique differences and the best ways to handle them.

COMMON APPROACH

Whether you're facing a conflict with a co-worker, your boss or a customer, there is a set of best practices to follow:

- **Keep your professionalism.** Stay calm and resist the temptation to give in to your emotions. If someone is yelling at you or making demeaning remarks, it's easy to return the favour and lash out at them. If you do that, the two of you will appear to other people like unprofessional people behaving immaturely. In Eckhart Tolle's book, *The Power of Now*, he talks about handling your emotions and controlling the urge to lash out (Tolle, 1992). While it may make you feel good temporarily when you lash out, it may damage your chances in the long run of having good working relationships.

The first step is to acknowledge the emotion you're feeling, such as anger. Just acknowledging your feelings will help you calm down and reduce your urge to strike back. Also keep in mind that when you let your emotions dictate your actions, you are giving your "power" to the other person. Ask yourself if the other person is that powerful for you to lose your control and give him the power over your reaction. The answer is most likely no. Avoid an unnecessary emotional confrontation by walking away, even for just a few minutes. Take deep breaths to calm yourself down. If you're not familiar with this kind of self-control practice, continue to patiently work on it, and over time you will gain more emotional discipline.

From my experience, taking a step back helps to clear my mind and allows me to dissect and clarify the situation. This may lower the "temperature", enable us to defuse a tense situation, and maybe allow us to reach a viable solution.

- **Focus on listening.** When faced with a conflict, we have a tendency to jump to conclusions and solutions right away without understanding first. Lack of communication or miscommunication often is the root of conflict. When people are talking over each other instead of stepping back and listening to what the other person is saying, confusion and misunderstanding can arise. Then as things escalate, they become more personal, emotional and before they know it, things have blown up into a real conflict. Sometimes what we thought we heard is not what the other person meant. To avoid this, ask: "What I hear you say is ABC... Did I hear correctly?" or "Can you give me an example...?" When you ask for clarification, you put the onus on that person to explain. Moreover, when people see that you're listening, they feel assured they're being heard, and this helps create a good communication channel which encourages them to be open to your views.

- **Prepare as best you can.** In any conflict or difficult situation, the more details we know about the situation, the better we are at keeping an open mind and being able to use our creativity to come up with the best solution possible. Some of the situational details include the nature of the conflict, possible causes, people involved, any impact on them and external factors. With the knowledge and information we have, we are in a better position to help get everyone on the same page and work to come up with the best solution. Spend time upfront to really understand the issue by talking and listening to the key stakeholders.

- **Use a logical problem-solving approach.** The first step in solving any problem is to define clearly what the problem is. It's not uncommon to see some people on the team trying to solve a problem while others have a different understanding of what the problem is. It's important to make sure everyone has the same understanding. This misunderstanding happens often in business negotiations where one party is working on one issue while the other party is focusing on a different one. Secondly, once the problem is understood, find out possible causes of the problem. The third step is to work with key stakeholders to brainstorm possible solutions and weigh the pros and cons of the different options. And finally, choose the best option among the ones considered.

HOW TO DEAL WITH DIFFICULT SITUATIONS

Now, let's look at several different scenarios and discuss them in more detail using the suggested approach above.

1. **Difficult customer.** A customer is unhappy because your company didn't meet its commitment and they may make life difficult for you when you meet them. It may be obvious but needs to be repeated that it's especially important to be professional and use your listening skills in this situation. Let the customer vent; listen and make sure you understand their issues. Moreover, when you interact with them, remember you're representing your company and not just the department you work in. Avoid blaming others in the company or being defensive that the customer is taking it out on you when it's not your fault. The customer doesn't care about your company problems and since you represent the company, you need to answer to the customer. Moreover, you need to be clear on the resolution or the next steps before

you leave the meeting and make sure you follow up accordingly.

Let me repeat a story I told in the "How to communicate and present to different audiences" chapter. I once took a customer visit trip with the purpose of getting their input on a future printer technology. Per my request, the account Sales Representative (SR) set up the meeting for me. When a co-worker and I arrived and met a couple of executives from the customer's company, they proceeded to lay into us about issues they had with their computer systems and their dissatisfaction with our company. We could sense their frustration and anger as the volume of their voices got louder. We were caught completely by surprise since we had no prior warnings from the SR. To make the situation worse, he wasn't there to handle these issues with the customer and since we were from the printer business unit, we were in the dark about their computer system issues. There was only one thing we could do – we sat down and listened patiently. We asked questions to make sure we captured their problems accurately. When they were done venting and giving us a list of items they wanted answers on, we calmly thanked them for their feedback. We told them that although we were not involved in these issues, we would make sure that the right people from the company would work on their request and get back to them quickly.

After this resolution, the customers felt their concerns were heard and were satisfied with the next steps. They calmed down, listened and discussed our company printing technology and even spent an extra hour with us on this topic. I also learned a good lesson from this visit: I should have talked with the SR to understand more about the customer and any potential issues I needed to be aware of and to address before I met them.

2. **Work conflict/difficult situation with co-workers.** One typical scenario here is you and other people are working on a project in which everyone's work is an important part of the overall project and if one person delivers subpar work, the whole project would be negatively impacted. You discover a co-worker's deliverables are not up to the team's standard. You want to let him know but you also know he has a big ego, is sensitive to criticism and does not have to answer to you. What do you do?

We'll apply the approach we discussed at beginning of this chapter. In this situation, focus on the business issue at hand. The key here is trying to understand, giving constructive feedback and emphasizing his ownership of the team's goals.

Approach the person to confirm or clarify his understanding of the team's goals to make sure that you are both on the same page. If he doesn't have the same understanding of the team goals, that could indicate the root cause of the problem. The team project's goals should be clearly written and communicated to everyone on the team. Go over these goals with him if you need to. Before discussing his specific work, ask for his feedback on the status of the team project and suggestions for improvement. Then tell him you have some constructive feedback and suggestions for his work. The key word here is constructive feedback, not negative criticism. Again, focus your feedback on his work and not him as a person. Give specific examples. For example: "The ROI analysis was missing key assumptions to validate the results" as opposed to "You completely missed the boat on the ROI analysis." Emphasize to him that everyone's work is critical to the overall project and if someone doesn't deliver their best work, the whole team suffers. Then offer your help and close the meeting with the timeline for him to review his work with the team again. If your message doesn't get through, suggest to him that the team may need to ask management for help to make sure they deliver the best results possible.

Let's take another real-life example related to me by a friend and former colleague. Henry worked as software (SW) Test Engineer on an engineering team. The team was on the hook to deliver and launch a new application on schedule. When going through the testing, Henry discovered the program was buggy and had logic errors. One of the SW programmers he needed cooperation from was very protective of his work and sensitive to criticism. Tom, a senior SW engineer, had been with the company for several years and believed there was nothing wrong with his work.

He didn't want to cooperate and would get offended if the test team approached him about his software code. The test team thought it was possible the issue could be his code but not sure. How would you handle this situation? Would you take him to the woodshed and read him the riot act? Or would you escalate the matter to management immediately and force him to cooperate.

I asked Henry how he handled this situation. He said he approached this with an open mind without assuming that the issue was Tom's code. He dealt with this difficult situation professionally and focused only on the business issue. He approached Tom to explain that the overall program was not working and it was critical to find out the root causes so the problem could be fixed. Henry then asked him for his thoughts on the possible causes and how to go about diagnosing the software bugs. This assuaged Tom from getting defensive or feeling he was being blamed. At the same time, Henry put the onus on him to get involved. Tom's demeanour changed and he suggested a couple of good ideas to go about discovering the bugs, including comprehensive integration testing of everyone's code. Henry then confirmed with Tom that the testing would include his code as well. The lesson here is by focusing on the business problem and having Tom involved in helping find the solution, Henry was successful in addressing this sensitive issue with him.

HOW TO HANDLE CONFLICTS

Let's assume despite all the effort from Henry, Tom remained stubborn and uncooperative. I would suggest the next step is to escalate the issue to management for help. Henry should also let Tom know he is bringing the situation to management. At least Tom would be in no position to complain since Henry is not going behind his back and he knows Henry had tried his best reaching out to him.

Regarding my situation where my co-worker Jim was blaming me and throwing me under the bus, it was just as easy for me to point fingers back at him and get into a pissing contest. However, I chose to keep my cool and waited until he had yelled enough. Then I calmly told him that the yelling was unprofessional and wasn't going to solve the problem. I then told him we needed to find the root causes so we could fix them. And if it turned out it was my work, then I would be happy to acknowledge my error and fix it. He was taken somewhat aback that I didn't lash back at him and he seemed a bit embarrassed. After working together for the next couple of days, we were able to diagnose the problem, fix it and move the project forward. The next day, he apologized to me for his outburst. After that incident, Jim was more aware of his behaviour and controlled his emotions better, at least with me. We continued to have a good professional working relationship. By not reacting badly back at him, I gave him an out and that enabled us to continue our working relationship. I was in control of the situation.

3. Conflict or difficult situation with your boss. A conflict arises when your boss assigns you additional work when you are completely swamped. You might feel upset that your boss doesn't appreciate you have too much work already. You may feel you're being taken advantage of and your boss doesn't care he's driving you too hard. You don't want to take on this new assignment. How would you handle this?

Treat this as a negotiation session on how to say no. The key again is to focus on the business issue and not get personal or emotional. Don't assume your boss knows how much work you have on your plate. Give him the benefit of the doubt. He is likely busy and not always able to keep tabs on your workload. The way to approach this is to give your boss visibility of your workload and have him prioritize for you. This gets him involved in solving the issue with you.

First, explain all the tasks you have on your plate, the effort and time they require, and be clear with him that it is not possible for you to take on more. However, you would be happy to take this work on if you can drop something else off your plate. Next, ask him to prioritize how important his request is relative to your current tasks. This forces him to evaluate carefully. If he prioritizes his request higher than your other assignments, then it would be reasonable to delay or drop the less important priorities. You need to be firm on this – if you take it on, something has to go. Or if he sees that his request isn't important enough, he can assign it to someone else who may not have as much going on.

4. **Pressure situation with executives.** There will be times in meetings when management may grill you with tough questions or challenge your work. Normally, they're not doing this to be mean to you. Rather, they want to test if you have done your homework, thought things through and can back it up. How well you prepare for meetings like this will determine how you perform. If you are prepared, you will come to the meeting with confidence and that will carry you through. Refer to the "How to communicate and present to specific audiences" and "How to create presentation content" chapters to help you prepare and conduct yourself in meetings.

To prepare for answering questions from executives, put yourself in their shoes and ask what tough questions you would ask yourself. Since you know the content of your material, think about where you are vulnerable and where the potential holes or weaknesses are. Ask yourself tough questions about those areas and figure out how you would answer them. Executives tend to see the big picture and ask open-ended questions such as: "Where do you see the risks of your project?", "What if things don't go as planned?"," What is your contingency plan?", "What are your key assumptions?", "What key stakeholders have you talked to?" and "What are the key requirements to achieve success?" Some executives are number-centric and will focus on your analysis to test for discrepancies. While you can't anticipate every question, preparing yourself with these questions and answers will give you the confidence and ability to think on your feet when you get a question you had not thought of.

If you get questions from the executives, don't appear ruffled, even if you feel tense and nervous. Remind yourself that you have done your best to prepare and to project confidence. Appearing timid or unsure about your recommendation will not inspire confidence in the executives. Even if you're coming to the meeting not fully prepared and hoping the management team will give you a pass, you need to do your best to maintain your poise. Here are some ways to handle yourself professionally in this type of situation.

▷ If you get a question where you don't know the answer off-hand but can get the answer later, you could say: "Good question. I don't have the answer off the top of my head but I can find out and get back to you after this meeting." That is a perfectly fine answer.

▷ If you are asked to give an opinion but you want to think about it before answering, you can buy some time. For example: "Great question. I'd like to give that some thought. Can I think about it a little bit and get back to you?" While the meeting is going on, you can think about that question in the back of your mind and get back to the questioner later in the meeting when ready. This is a good and professional way to handle this type of question.

▷ If an executive expresses doubt about your analysis or recommendation, don't get defensive. Focus on the business issue. Ask for clarification from the executive, such as: "Can you help me understand the specific area of your concern?" or "What I heard is that you're not sure about my conclusion on ABC because I didn't show enough data to support it, is that right?" When you get the clarification, you will more likely be able to respond better. Don't get flustered when they push you. Sometimes they want to see how strong your conviction is on the recommendation. If you did not have enough data or analysis to support your argument, acknowledge their question and propose to come back with more analysis. For example: "Thank you for the question. Let me look into this further and get back to you with a more detailed analysis."

▷ If an executive starts to drill down on your data, try not to get dragged down this path. It's a no-win situation and distracts everyone from the meeting's objective. Instead of focusing on the results, focus on your assumptions. For example, you may say: "Since the outcomes of the analysis are the results of the assumptions, let me show you my assumptions to get your thoughts and we can debate on the validity of these assumptions." By definition, assumptions are your educated guesses on the future or on the unknown, so they are not right or wrong at the moment. Therefore, the assumptions are open for debate and you can modify your analysis if the assumptions change. By handling things this way, you're being mature and professional, and you show you are open to people's opinions. If some assumptions need to be modified, thank the executives and say you will look at the analysis again based on the new assumptions. In this process, you have gotten the executives to get involved and take some ownership of your work.

5. **How to handle surprises in real time.** Last-minute surprises are toughest to handle. One of my former companies hosts an annual customer event where a couple hundred executives from Fortune 1000 companies are invited to come for updates on the company's future plan and strategy. We usually offer simultaneous sessions for the guests to choose which ones to attend. One year, our server business unit was allocated a big portion of the agenda to present to customers and we planned to have three speakers for this talk – two co-workers and me. On the morning of the presentation, the two co-workers were nowhere to be found. Moreover, the presentation materials the team worked on were on their laptops. We received no answer calling their hotel rooms or cell phones. Then we received a 15-minute heads-up and my manager was now in full panic

mode. We asked another business unit to present in our time slot but they weren't ready either.

Out of desperation, I told a Sales Account Manager I had worked with about our predicament and asked her if she had any ideas. She thought for a couple of minutes and then suggested I could buy some time by opening the session and inviting the customers to give feedback on any topics they wanted. And it would be a great opportunity for the company top executives to hear their feedback directly. That was as good of an idea as any and I informed my boss of the plan. To my pleasant surprise, the feedback discussion went on for over an hour and was so successful I had a difficult time stopping the customer discussion so we could proceed with our presentation. The two missing speakers finally made it there after 30 minutes into the session. Afterwards, many of the customers thanked my boss and even suggested that every future session should allocate time for customer feedback. We heaved a sigh of relief because of how close we cut it.

The lesson learned here is to think of possible unexpected events and to prepare for them as best you can. And if it does happen, stay calm and keep your poise in order to think creatively and engage the right people for help. These are just some real-life examples of typical difficult situations you may face at work and while there will be many other situations you'll encounter throughout your career, keep in mind the Common Approach I described above: keep your professionalism; focus on listening; prepare as best you can; and use a logical problem-solving approach. Applying this Common Approach strategy to any challenging situation you face will give you a greater chance to solve it effectively, gain credibility and trust, and establish yourself as a true professional who's unruffled and poised in any pressure circumstances.

How to Deal with Difficult Co-workers

While we all want a friendly and productive work environment, there are people of all types and personalities, and the difficult ones can make things uncomfortable and not fun for other workers. For the most part, we cannot control people or choose whom to work with. It's easy to work with reasonable, professional colleagues who put team goals first. However, if we know how to handle these difficult workers, it reduces the frustration and more importantly, allows us to get our work done while keeping the work environment as friendly and enjoyable as possible. In this chapter, I'll cover effective ways to manage and deal with difficult co-workers.

1. **Party Pooper.** This person is Mr No. He presents an impediment to what you want to do. He doesn't like anything he sees and shoots down your work. He looks for what can go wrong with your plan and potential negative outcomes. While it can be useful to have a set of critical eyes examining your idea, he only sees failure, and does not offer constructive feedback or useful suggestions. His main message is that your plan has no chance to succeed. His

How to Deal with Difficult Co-workers: Suggested Responses

Party pooper

Mr "No!"

→ Need to stand up
→ Ask for specific input
→ Follow-up closely

Downer

Sees mostly the negative side

→ Listen but don't be down

Bully

Intimidates, threatens, strong-arms

→ Avoid engaging emotionally
→ Ask for specific input on task
→ Highlight request to manager

Bragger

Exaggerates and name-drops

→ Look beyond BS for content

Exploiter

Takes advantage of others

→ Avoid distractions with negative impact on own job performance
→ Be clear and firm on own priorities

One-upper

Needs to step on you to look better

→ Seek clarity on critique
→ Let objective stakeholder judge

Gossiper

Negative and not focused on work

→ Avoid distraction and feeding into his acts
→ Speak to him if a rumour is about you
→ Seek clarifications and engage direct with the source of information

Hidden dragon

Fails to respond

→ Request clearly in writing
→ Set clear timeline and cc team/manager
→ Track timeline with reminders and escalation

Avoider

Does the bare minimum

→ Set fair and clear actions from him
→ Track timeline and escalate if needed

"Yes Boss" only

Responds depending on your rank

→ Request clearly in writing, including team
→ Track timeline with team reminders and escalations to boss

comments can be condescending, for example: "You did not think this through."

With this type of person, you need to stand up to him. However, stay calm and keep it professional by focusing on the issue. The best way to respond is to put the ball in his court and force him to respond to the topic at hand instead of just shooting down your plan. For example: "Give me specific examples of my plan that you don't think are good", and wait to hear from him. If he's being vague, repeat your question again with: "I can't improve on my plan unless I can get specific examples from you." If he gives you some useful examples, thank him and follow up with: "Can you give me suggestions on how I can improve my proposal?" If he asks to get back to you later, be sure to follow up with him. If he was just shooting off his mouth, he looks foolish and loses credibility.

2. **Downer.** This person is not a happy person generally and lives by the motto "Misery loves company". She is a glass-half-empty kind of person who looks at the negative side of things. For example, when company management is having an employee communication meeting, she tends to draw negative observations and cast suspicion on management's intention. Being around this person too much can bring you down and make the work environment less enjoyable. This type of person wants to draw you into their company and share their negative attitude.

Since people like to be listened to, try to listen for a little bit but don't get drawn into a conversation. You can say something like: "That's an interesting point and I didn't think of it like that, but I would rather talk about something else." Or if you feel the need to refute her, say: "I hear what you're saying, but I really didn't take it the same way." Or if you have more time, you can ask for specifics: "Give me an example of why you feel this way." Responses like these let the person know that while you want to listen and understand where they are coming from, you have a different view. Then ask to talk later since you need to get back to work.

3. **Bully.** This person uses strong-arm tactics. Intimidation, thinly veiled threats, pressure and name-dropping are some tactics he uses. He tells you if you don't do what he says, bad things will happen to you. Your job performance will take a hit, you will be perceived negatively by other managers or he will let important people in the company know it was your fault the work didn't get done. He tends to come across as having power, self-perceived power, over you and other people and as being well connected in the company.

While it's easy to get angry and let this person get on your nerves, or worse, you feel intimidated or victim-ized, do your best to resist this. You may feel the urge to tell this person to take a hike, but there are better ways to handle him. Similar to the above example, stay professional by addressing the issue at hand and nothing else. Remind yourself that he's not worth wasting your energy on. A good response technique is to pepper him with questions to force him to be explicitly clear on the what's and the why's. This way you let him know you're not intimidated and won't just follow his instructions blindly. Ask him for the specifics of the task – why the need to do this, what problem he is trying to solve, what the goals are, and why this task is more important than other tasks that are being worked on. Force him to answer these tough questions. It's also important for you to understand how this request fits into the priorities that you and your manager have agreed on. Then with confidence, you can say no by explaining this doesn't fit into your priorities at the moment. However, if you think this is a big-enough deal, be sure to let your manager know in case it comes back to your manager later. If the Bully pulls the name-dropping card or uses threats, calmly tell him that you will be more than happy to discuss this with your manager and together will make the call on the priority. Then discuss this with your manager.

4. **Bragger.** As the name implies, this person is a talker who is all about "me", who likes to brag about himself, puts himself in the centre of attention, and has a tendency to embellish and exaggerate. He's also prone to name-dropping to show his importance, but generally is harmless, although he can be quite annoying.

The trick here is to look beyond the braggadocio, focus on the substance and judge the value of the content yourself. Ask for facts and tangible results and don't take his words at face value. When it's not a topic related to you, just ignore him. There's no need to set him straight or make his head any bigger.

5. **Exploiter.** This person takes advantage of your generosity. Once you helped her, she'll keep coming back, knocking on your door with more requests for help. She can appear needy, making self-pitying comments, and is especially good at making you feel guilty if you turn her down – "If you don't help me with this, I'll get in big trouble with my boss." This person uses your generous nature against you to get you to do what she wants.

As much as we like to help and don't like to say no, there are times we need to say no because otherwise, we can't get our work done and it will negatively impact our own job performance. If we were to help someone complete their task but got behind on our work or delivered less than stellar results, we only hurt ourselves and would get no credit for helping others. Remember, before we can help people, we need to take care of our own job first. I would suggest listening to the request, then telling her you empathise with her situation, but your plate is full with tight deadlines and your manager wants you to focus on these priorities first. As a result, you cannot help but you may have more time later when you finish your work. Be firm with your answer.

6. **One-upper.** This person has a need to be better than you, especially if you are in a similar job. No matter how good your work is, she needs to find weak spots to pick on. This trait is a little bit similar to the "Party Pooper", but this person is not just critiquing your idea but also wants to show that her work is better. You would hear comments such as: "I don't see clear benefits of your plan," "This plan is confusing," "This plan requires too much time to implement," or "It's not very useful."

Let me share with you an example. The pricing team at a previous company developed a tool that allowed the users – Product Managers (PMs) – to easily and quickly run different pricing scenarios and compare the results. This tool was best for "what if" analysis, a key part of a PM's role. Previously it would take days to run this kind of analysis, and now it would take minutes to see the results, thus saving a huge amount of time. However, it would require the PMs to invest some initial time to learn how to use the tool. When the pricing manager, Mark, explained the features of the tool to the product management team, one of the managers in the meeting, Jane, shot it down, saying: "This tool is really complex and difficult to use and is not foolproof and prone to people making mistakes." Jane then brought up her own tool she has been using and compared against the pricing team's tool. It turned out her tool was good for her own specific use but not for other PMs, whereas the pricing team's tool was designed for multiple uses by different people.

The way to respond to this person is to seek clarity of their critique first. Avoid getting defensive. Instead, focus on the subject matter. If it turns out that their work is better or can improve yours, acknowledge and thank them. Otherwise, let others make the comparison and decide. From my example above, after asking Jane for more details, the pricing manager explained that his goal was to create a tool that met different needs of the Product Managers, and they should use whichever tool was best for them. Then he opened up the discussion to get other people's feedback. A couple of managers thought the pricing tool was a good fit for their needs and they didn't think it was too complex. In addition, they also thought Jane's tool was too limited for their needs. They then suggested having their teams try both tools and then give an assessment after a few days. After the testing was finished, they chose the pricing team's tool. The key point here is to let objective stakeholders be the judge.

7. **Gossiper.** This person talks to you about other people and maybe to other people about you. He likes to start or spread rumours and engage in conspiracy theories. The gossip often is personal. He sometimes pits people against each other. Even on company issues, the Gossiper often engages in

company rumours such as potential reorganizations, firings and promotions. Although the gossip can be about any number of things, most of them tend to be negative. This person doesn't seem to focus on the work at hand but enjoys mingling with people. This not only makes you feel uncomfortable, but also distracts you from doing your work.

The way to deal with this person is to avoid engaging if you can. If you have no choice but to listen for a few minutes, just listen but don't participate. Don't give your opinion or ask for more details. Look for a break in the conversation and excuse yourself to go back to your work. If you really feel uncomfortable about the topic and don't want to hear the gossip, just be honest and say you prefer not to know because it makes you uncomfortable.

If you find out from reliable sources that the Gossiper has been gossiping bad things about you to other people, one way to handle this is to confront him directly but professionally. State that you heard from other people what he had said about you and you want to confirm if that is true. If he admits it, ask for clarifications. Regardless of the explanation, you can be direct by saying that you absolutely prefer to talk directly with people who have things to say about you, that you welcome and want to hear feedback but not second-hand. Moreover, express that in the future if he has something to say to you, even negative things, you would like him to talk to you directly.

8. Hidden Dragon. This person disappears, remains silent and doesn't get back to you on your question, message or inquiry. She does not keep you updated on her work progress that impacts you and she doesn't share relevant information with you. For example, you send her an email message asking for a date that she can give you the result of her work so you can do yours. One day, two days, three days go by and no answer. You resend the message and still no response. You see her in the hallway, ask her about it and she says she will get back to you. We can speculate why she is this way – maybe she is absent-minded, disorganized, inconsiderate or irresponsible, but whatever the reason is, it's not important to you.

The way to handle this person is make sure you have your question or message in writing. If she was assigned an action item that you depend on, make sure the deliverables and the due date are clear to her. Send a confirmation message to her, copy other team members and her manager. The day before the due date, forward your previous message to her with a reminder of the action items and due date. She may find this annoying but will get the message. If she still doesn't deliver, you can escalate to her manager and you have evidence to support your escalation.

9. Avoider. This person is a master of delegating work to others, deflecting his responsibilities and not taking accountability. He's good at coming up with excuses to avoid taking on action items. He does the minimum to get by and is prone to point fingers when something goes wrong. He may also use "Not in my work scope" to avoid doing tasks. He only has his own interests at heart and is uncooperative in areas not totally aligned with his personal interests.

Similar to the "Hidden Dragon", clear and written communication is key to dealing with this person. If you are the project lead or even just a team member, make sure that the work is assigned fairly and everyone has action items. The way to handle his attempt at avoiding work is to give him a choice: "We all have to share the work, so you can take on action item #1 or action item #2," and you move on only after this is decided. Then make sure the expected results and deadlines are clear. Summarize all the action items and send a summary message to him, copying team members and his manager.

10. **"Yes Boss" Only.** Hierarchy motivation drives his action with "rank" in mind. He only listens respectfully to the boss or higher-ranking managers. And then he turns around and is nasty with other co-workers. He often takes credit for work done by others and is good at hiding this character trait from his superiors.

The key here is to keep paper trails. On important things and work you've completed and want to share with your colleagues and managers, write and send out email messages, copying relevant people. Since this type of person tends to avoid challenging work, follow the suggestion from #9. Make sure he's assigned appropriate tasks and hold his feet to fire.

These are just some real-life examples of typical difficult colleagues you may face at work. Keep in mind some key points in dealing with these situations: focus on the business problem at hand and not let it turn into a personal conflict, keep your professionalism and try your best to not lose your cool, putting the onus on that person to give examples. You will come across as an ultimate professional who is effective in working with different colleagues to get work done.

About the Authors

Dennis Mark has more than 30 years of experience in the Information Technology industry, holding senior leadership positions including Vice President and General Manager of Solutions & Services for HP Inc Asia Pacific. In his international consulting capacity, he provides business subject matter expertise supporting organisational development, critical research and business decisions.

Michael Dam is an Adjunct Lecturer at Santa Clara University, California. He conducts career talks at universities as well as teaching career workshops, and provides individual coaching to career professionals. Michael holds an MBA and participated in the prestigious Accelerated Executive Leadership Program at Stanford University.

Dennis Mark and Michael Dam's 2022 publication, *Thriving At Work: What School Doesn't Teach You*, was lauded as "an absolute gem" and "a must-have career 101 handbook".

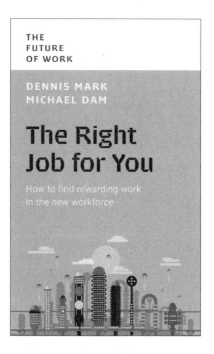

THE
FUTURE
OF WORK

DENNIS MARK
MICHAEL DAM

The Right Job for You

How to find rewarding work
in the new workforce

In the new world of work, old jobs are being disrupted or eliminated just as new ones are being invented that never existed before. On top of that, professionals are not only changing jobs, but even changing careers over the course of their working life.

Here is a timely and much-needed guide to finding – and securing – the job opportunities that will bring you financial and personal fulfilment in this highly fluid business landscape. From exploring the roles most suited to your skillsets, to crafting the strategies for landing a coveted position, *The Right Job For You* will set you up for success!

THE
FUTURE
OF WORK

DENNIS MARK
MICHAEL DAM

Powerful Work Hacks

How to work smarter, faster and healthier with future-ready skills

Remote working, automation, co-working spaces, diversity and inclusion – the workplace is undergoing unprecedented change. In order to stay not just relevant, but productive and successful, today's professionals will need to upgrade their work practices and skills.

Powerful Work Hacks presents you with highly effective "hacks" that can be put into practice right away. These tools are designed to improve personal productivity, increase job fulfilment, promote mental well-being, accelerate career growth, and ensure future-readiness.